D0533127

**POCKET EYEWITNESS**

# ROCKS AND MINERALS

# FACTS AT YOUR FINGERTIPS

**DK DELHI**
**Project editor** Bharti Bedi
**Project art editor** Deep Shikha Walia
**Senior editor** Kingshuk Ghoshal
**Senior art editor** Govind Mittal
**Assistant art editor** Aanchal Singal
**Jacket designer** Juhi Sheth
**Jackets editorial coordinator** Priyanka Sharma
**DTP designers** Rajesh Singh Adhikari,
Jaypal Singh Chauhan
**Picture researcher** Sumedha Chopra
**Managing editor** Saloni Talwar
**Managing art editor** Romi Chakraborty
**CTS manager** Balwant Singh
**Production manager** Pankaj Sharma

**DK LONDON**
**Senior editor** Fleur Star
**Senior art editor** Philip Letsu
**Jacket designer** Surabhi Wadhwa
**Jacket editor** Claire Gell
**Jacket design development manager**
Sophia MTT
**Production editor** Ben Marcus
**Production controller** Mary Slater

**Publisher** Andrew Macintyre
**Associate publishing director** Liz Wheeler
**Art director** Phil Ormerod
**Publishing director** Jonathan Metcalf

**Consultant** Kevin Walsh

This edition published in 2018
First published in Great Britain in 2012 by
Dorling Kindersley Limited
80 Strand, London, WC2R 0RL

A CIP catalogue record for this book
is available from the British Library.

ISBN: 978-0-2413-4367-8

Printed and bound in China

A WORLD OF IDEAS:
**SEE ALL THERE IS TO KNOW**

www.dk.com

# CONTENTS

**Scales and sizes**
This book contains profiles of rocks and minerals with scale drawings to indicate their size.

15 cm
(6 in)

# Our rocky planet

Our planet is like an onion, made up of a number of layers. In the centre is a solid core, which is surrounded by the mantle and the crust. We live on Earth's surface on top of the crust, the thin outer layer that carries oceans and continents. These layers developed early in Earth's history. During Earth's formation, denser materials, such as iron, sank to the centre, while lighter materials, such as silicates and other minerals, rose to the surface.

**Upper mantle** is made of warm, mobile rocks

## Core and mantle

The core is made up of a solid inner part and a liquid outer part. The mantle is a layer of dense minerals, just above the core. High pressure makes the lower mantle solid, while the minerals in the upper mantle are like a gluey liquid. Molten rocks found inside Earth are called magma.

**Lower mantle** contains dense rock formed under pressure

**Outer core** creates Earth's magnetic field as the molten material moves

**Inner core** is solid and contains a mixture of iron and nickel

**Atmosphere** consists of gases

**Crust** is made of solid rock, and forms oceans and continents

The oldest type of rock is Acasta gneiss, which first formed 4.2 billion years ago.

Lava flowing today from Kilauea volcano, Hawaiian Islands, will cool to form igneous rocks.

## How old are rocks?

Rocks formed when Earth was cool enough for them to become solid. The first rock on Earth solidified around 4.2 billion years ago. Rocks and minerals have been forming ever since and are still forming today – at Earth's surface, in the crust, on the ocean floor, and in the mantle deep below.

## Earth's crust

The crust is made up of panels" called tectonic plates. When two plates collide, they push against one another, sometimes forming mountains. This tectonic movement may bring up rocks from deep inside the mantle to the surface.

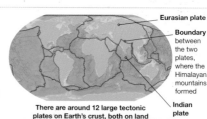

**Eurasian plate**

**Boundary** between the two plates, where the Himalayan mountains formed

**Indian plate**

There are around 12 large tectonic plates on Earth's crust, both on land and below the seas and oceans.

# What is a mineral?

A mineral is a naturally occurring, solid inorganic substance, which means it doesn't come from the remains of plants or animals. It is made from chemical elements – simple substances that cannot be broken down further. Minerals grow or cement together to form rocks.

Green chrysocolla is a mineral

## What is a mineral made of?

Minerals are chemical compounds made up of two or more chemical elements. The atoms in the elements bind together to form solid pieces called crystals. Some crystals can grow to several metres wide, but others are so tiny they can only be seen with a microscope.

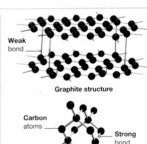

Weak bond

**Graphite structure**

Carbon atoms

Strong bond

**Diamond structure**

When crystals have enough room to grow, they form **well-defined shapes**, such as seen in this amethyst.

## Pattern of atoms

The atoms of elements in a mineral form a s pattern that never changes. This pattern giv the mineral its properties, such as hardness, colour, and shape. For example, graphite an diamond are both forms of carbon. In graph the atoms are linked with weak bonds, which makes it soft. Diamond has strong bonds, making it the hardest mineral.

Feldspar in granite

## rock-forming minerals

eralogists (people who study minerals) metimes group minerals into two types: ore nerals and rock-forming minerals. This group ludes feldspar, which is one of the most undant of all minerals and is found in many es of rock.

## re minerals

me minerals are mined for their metal ntent. Known as ore minerals, they are ushed and separated and then refined and elted to produce metal. This LKAB mine in eden is the largest in the world. Most of its e is magnetite, which is used to produce iron.

### MINERAL OR NOT?

Although some substances such as **oil** may be called minerals, they come from the remains of living things and are actually classified as hydrocarbons.

Oil rig, North Sea

**Minerals** such as rubies, diamonds, and emeralds can be copied and produced in laboratories. Such artificial versions are not true minerals because they do not grow naturally.

Artificial rubies

# What is a rock?

A rock is a solid collection of mineral grains that grow or become cemented together. Geologists (people who study rocks and minerals) classify rocks into three main types on the basis of how they are formed – igneous, sedimentary, and metamorphic.

## Composition

Every rock is made up of one or more minerals. For example, gabbro, an igneous rock, is made up of minerals including olivine, pyroxene, and plagioclase feldspar.

**Plagioclase feldspar**
The light grains are a type of feldspar called plagioclase. There are different kinds of feldspar minerals, which form part of most types of rock.

Gabbro

**Olivine**
This mineral forms only in igneous rocks that solidify below the ground. It contains iron and magnesium.

**Thin slice of gabbro seen under a microscope**

**Pyroxene**
This mineral is abundant in Earth's mantle. Some rocks on the Moon are also made of pyroxene.

# TYPES OF ROCK

**Igneous rocks** form from molten magma that has cooled and hardened on or below Earth's surface.

**Obsidian is an igneous rock**

**Red colour** due to iron oxide

**Red sandstone is a sedimentary rock**

**Sedimentary rocks** form at Earth's surface and consist of layers of rock fragments, minerals, or organic matter such as sea shells that have been deposited on top of each other.

**Metamorphic rocks** can form when rocks are squeezed by pressure and heated deep under Earth's crust.

**Banded gneiss is a metamorphic rock**

# Be a collector

Rocks and minerals can be found everywhere – up in the mountains, along streams, on beaches, and even on a driveway! Collecting them and recording the finds is a popular hobby that dates back to the 19th century.

## Safety first

Protective clothing and shoes may need to be worn at certain collection sites. Rocks can splinter while chipping or trimming, so it is best to wear protective goggles and gloves. A compass and a map are useful for directions.

Map and compass

Protective gloves

Hard

Goggles

## In the field

Before going out in the field to collect rocks, it is a good idea to find out about the site and the kind of specimens expected to be found there. Joining a group of collectors can be more fun and is safer than taking the trip alone.

**Paint brush** for cleaning specimens

**Pocket knife**

**Sieve** for sorting rocks from sand

**Trowel** for digging soft rocks

**Geological hammer** with a rubber grip

**Wide-ended chisel** for splitting rocks

## ssential tools

ile collecting rocks and minerals in the field, a
ge of tools are required. These include a chisel
a geological hammer. A regular hammer may
nter the rock or the mineral specimen dangerously.

## eeping records

ome cases, it is better to observe and record
nples with a camera or in a sketchpad than
ove them from a site, which may damage the
ks. The exact location and details of a find
be recorded in a notebook.

**Notebook** for noting specimen details

**Digital camera**

**Bubble wrap** to carry specimens

## Handle with care

To collect a sample
of a rock or a mineral,
chip or trim it to size with
a hammer. Wrap it in a
newspaper or a bubble wrap
to keep it scratch-free.

## Cleaning specimens

Most specimens are dirty when collected. Surplus rock fragments can be removed from a specimen by washing in water. A gentle scrub with a brush helps remove loose soil and debris when the specimen is dry. Every specimen must be cleaned only as much as needed. It is best to begin with the most gentle method.

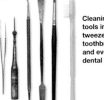

Cleaning tools include tweezers, toothbrushes, and even dental picks

**Index cards** to list specimens alphabetically and store field notes or other details

## Labelling

After the specimens have been identified, label them for future reference, along with notes on their location or other specific details.

**Magnify glass** to study an identify

**Cotton** to clean specimens

**Plastic box**
for brittle pieces

## Storage and display

To avoid damage, specimens can be stored in individual trays or boxes. It is useful to keep an index for larger collections, using index cards to record details of the specimens, such as their locations and the dates of collection.

**Templates** to make cardboard boxes for storage

# Rocks

When minerals grow or cement together, they can form rocks. Some rocks, such as dolomite, are made up of only one mineral. However, most rocks are a combination of two or more minerals. Some also contain fossils of plants and animals. New rocks form in different ways – when magma becomes solid, when old rocks break down, or when there is a change in temperature or pressure.

**MOAI**
Found on Easter Island, the Moai are human figures carved out of pieces of rock called tuff.

# How rocks are made

Rocks are formed and destroyed all the time. There are three main ways rocks form. Igneous rocks form when magma and lava solidify. Sedimentary rocks form in layers made up of pieces of existing rock that have been broken down by erosion and weathering. Metamorphic rocks form by heat or pressure.

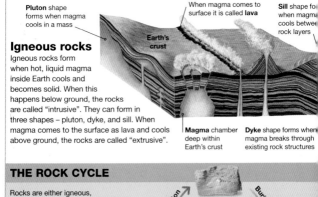

**Pluton** shape forms when magma cools in a mass

When magma comes to surface it is called **lava**

**Sill** shape for when magma cools betwee rock layers

Earth's crust

## Igneous rocks

Igneous rocks form when hot, liquid magma inside Earth cools and becomes solid. When this happens below ground, the rocks are called "intrusive". They can form in three shapes – pluton, dyke, and sill. When magma comes to the surface as lava and cools above ground, the rocks are called "extrusive".

**Magma chamber** deep within Earth's crust

**Dyke** shape forms when magma breaks through existing rock structures

## THE ROCK CYCLE

Rocks are either igneous, sedimentary, or metamorphic. Over thousands of years, rocks can change from one type to another, from igneous to sedimentary to metamorphic and back to igneous. This process is called the rock cycle.

Erosion

Sedimentary rock

Burial

Igneous rock

Metamorp rock

Melting

# edimentary rocks

limentary rocks form on, or
y near, Earth's surface where
ded rock particles
sported by wind,
er, and ice are
osited on dry
d, on the beds
vers and lakes,
in the seas.

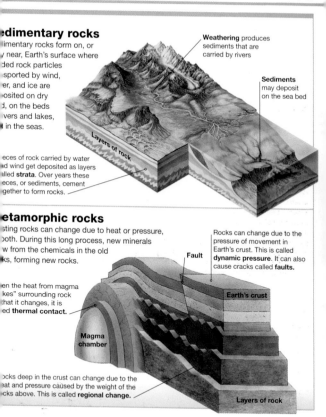

**Weathering** produces
sediments that are
carried by rivers

**Sediments**
may deposit
on the sea bed

Layers of rock

eces of rock carried by water
d wind get deposited as layers
lled **strata**. Over years these
eces, or sediments, cement
gether to form rocks.

# etamorphic rocks

sting rocks can change due to heat or pressure,
both. During this long process, new minerals
w from the chemicals in the old
ks, forming new rocks.

Rocks can change due to the
pressure of movement in
Earth's crust. This is called
**dynamic pressure**. It can also
cause cracks called **faults**.

**Fault**

**Earth's crust**

en the heat from magma
kes" surrounding rock
hat it changes, it is
ed **thermal contact**.

**Magma
chamber**

cks deep in the crust can change due to the
eat and pressure caused by the weight of the
cks above. This is called **regional change**.

**Layers of rock**

# Identifying rocks

Geologists can identify rocks through characteristics such as the size, shape, and arrangement of their grains. Grains in igneous roc are usually randomly arranged. Sedimentary rocks are made of roc particles and minerals that are cemented together. In metamorphic rocks, the grains are often aligned into patterns, known as foliation

## IGNEOUS ROCK CHARACTERISTICS

Peridotite

Basalt

Pink granite

### Large grains

Igneous rocks form below ground when magma in Earth's crust solidifies. The grains are well-developed and large as they have enough time to grow. Peridotite is an igneous rock with well-developed grains.

### Small grains

When magma erupts from volcanoes and reaches Earth's surface, it is called lava. When this lava solidifies above the ground, it cools down rapidly. This gives little time for grains to develop. Basalt is an example of an igneous rock with small grains.

### Colour

The mineral content of an igneous rock can be determined from its colou A light-coloured igneous rock, such as pink granite, is rich in silica. Dark-coloured rocks have less silica but contain othe dark, heavy minerals.

# SEDIMENTARY ROCK CHARACTERISTICS

Conglomerate

### Grain size

The grains in sedimentary rocks are of different sizes and textures. Conglomerate grains are coarse.

Millet-seed sandstone

### Grain shape

The shape of particles in sedimentary rocks show how the particles were transported. The particles of this sandstone were rounded by desert winds.

Freshwater limestone

### Presence of fossils

The presence of fossils is an indicator of rock type. They are very common in sedimentary rocks such as limestone, but rare in metamorphic rocks. Fossils never occur in igneous rocks.

# METAMORPHIC ROCK CHARACTERISTICS

Fine grain size

Marble

### Size of grains

Grains in metamorphic rocks grow slowly. Large grains indicate that the rock was formed under high pressure and heat. Rocks that form under lower pressure and heat have smaller grains.

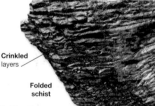

Crinkled layers

Folded schist

### Foliation

When a metamorphic rock forms under pressure, its grains may line up in patterns. This gives the rock a distinct wavy appearance.

# Igneous rocks

The Latin word *ignis* means "fire". Igneous rocks form when hot, molten magma inside Earth is pushed towards the crust and cools above or below the surface, forming solid rocks.

FOCUS ON...
**FORMATIONS**
Igneous rocks form some amazing natural structures, and man-made ones too.

## Obsidian

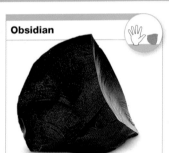

Obsidian forms when lava cools so rapidly that mineral crystals do not have time to grow. In ancient times, Native Americans, Aztecs, and Greeks used obsidian to make weapons, tools, and ornaments.

| | |
|---|---|
| **WHERE FORMED** | Above ground |
| **SHAPE WHEN FORMED** | Lava flow |
| **GRAIN SIZE** | Fine |
| **COLOUR** | Black, brown |
| **MINERAL CONTENT** | Glass |

## Basalt

When the lava cools and solidifies into basalt on Earth's surface, it may split into many-sided columns. Basalt forms ocean floors and large outcrops on land, such as the Deccan Traps, in India. It is rich in iron and magnesium.

| | |
|---|---|
| **WHERE FORMED** | Above ground |
| **SHAPE WHEN FORMED** | Lava flow |
| **GRAIN SIZE** | Fine to coarse |
| **COLOUR** | Dark grey to black |
| **MINERAL CONTENT** | Pyroxene, plagioclase, olivine, magnetite |

The Giant's Causeway, Northern Ireland, is 000 basalt pillars cked closely together.

▲ The Devil's Tower, made of phonolite, was declared a national monument of the USA in 1906.

▲ Sierra Nevada is a huge mass of granite, formed at great depth, brought to the surface.

▲ Mount Rushmore's granite has been carved to show the faces of American presidents.

## Granite

Granite is formed deep inside Earth's crust. It forms when magma cools down slowly. Crushed granite is used as gravel and road-building material. Polished granite is used for kitchen worktops and gravestones.

**WHERE FORMED**   Below ground

**SHAPE WHEN FORMED**   Pluton

**GRAIN SIZE**   Medium to coarse

**COLOUR**   White, light grey, grey, pink, red

**MINERAL CONTENT**   Feldspars, quartz, mica, hornblende

## Dolerite

Dolerite is an extremely hard rock and occurs in fissures in other rocks. You can see the crystals in dolerite with the naked eye.

**WHERE FORMED**   Below ground

**SHAPE WHEN FORMED**   Dykes, sills

**GRAIN SIZE**   Fine to medium

**COLOUR**   Dark grey to black, often mottled white

**MINERAL CONTENT**   Plagioclase, pyroxene, quartz, magnetite, olivine

## Diorite

A prized rock in ancient Egypt, diorite was used to build columns, figures, and sarcophagi (stone coffins), and for lining the chambers of some pyramids.

| | |
|---|---|
| **WHERE FORMED** | Below ground |
| **SHAPE WHEN FORMED** | Pluton, dyke, sill |
| **GRAIN SIZE** | Medium to coarse |
| **COLOUR** | Mottled black, dark green, grey, white |
| **MINERAL CONTENT** | Plagioclase, hornblende, biotite |

## Rhyolite

## Kimberlite

Kimberlite is the major source of diamonds. Kimberley in South Africa was one of the first sites to be mined for diamonds and inspired the name of the rock. However, not every occurrence yields gem-quality diamonds.

| | |
|---|---|
| **WHERE FORMED** | Below ground |
| **SHAPE WHEN FORMED** | Dyke, pipe |
| **GRAIN SIZE** | Fine to coarse |
| **COLOUR** | Dark grey |
| **MINERAL CONTENT** | Olivine, pyroxene, mica, garnet, ilmenite, diamond |

Rhyolite is a rare rock that forms from volcanic eruptions. Its lava is very rich in silica, so it is very sticky and may plug the volcano's vent.

**WHERE FORMED** Above ground

**SHAPE WHEN FORMED** Lava flow

**GRAIN SIZE** Fine to coarse

**COLOUR** Very light to medium grey, light pink

**MINERAL CONTENT** Quartz, potassium feldspar, glass, biotite, amphibole, plagioclase

# Peridotite

This rock forms much of Earth's mantle. Eruptions of magma from the mantle can bring up nodules (lumps) of peridotite to the surface. It is a major source of chromium.

Green olivine

**WHERE FORMED** Below ground

**SHAPE WHEN FORMED** Pluton, dyke, sill

**GRAIN SIZE** Coarse

**COLOUR** Dark green to black

**MINERAL CONTENT** Olivine, pyroxene, garnet, chromite

## ndesite

This rock is named after the Andes mountains of South America. It erupts from volcanoes and is found in areas where one tectonic plate slides under another, such as in the Andes.

**HERE FORMED** Above ground

**IAPE WHEN FORMED** Lava flow

**RAIN SIZE** Fine, with some small grains

**OLOUR** Light to dark grey, reddish-pink

**INERAL CONTENT** Feldspars, pyroxene, nphibole, biotite

## Pumice

Highly porous and frothlike, pumice forms when gas-filled liquid magma erupts like a fizzy drink from a shaken bottle and cools quickly. The resulting foam solidifies into a rock that is light enough to float on water.

**WHERE FORMED**  Above ground

**SHAPE WHEN FORMED**  Lava flow

**GRAIN SIZE**  Fine

**COLOUR**  White, yellow, grey, black

**MINERAL CONTENT**  Glass, feldspar, quartz

## Ignimbrite

This is a type of tuff that is deposited by flowing rivers of ash. Such flows can cause deaths during volcanic eruptions. In June 1912, Novarupta, a volcano in Alaska, produced the largest quantity of ignimbrite in history.

**WHERE FORMED**  Above ground

**SHAPE WHEN FORMED**  Lava flow

**GRAIN SIZE**  Fine

**COLOUR**  Pale cream, red-brown, grey

**MINERAL CONTENT**  Igneous rock and crystal fragments, welded volcanic glass

## Pélé's hair

Named after the Hawaiian goddess of fire, this rock has a fine, wispy texture. It forms when very liquid magma is spewed out from a volcano and cools rapidly in mid-air.

**WHERE FORMED**  Above ground

**SHAPE WHEN FORMED**  Lava spray

**GRAIN SIZE**  Very fine

**COLOUR**  Pale brown

**MINERAL CONTENT**  Basaltic glass

## uff

ff forms when foaming magma
mes up to the surface as
mixture of hot gases and
owing particles, and is
rown out from a volcano.

**HERE FORMED**  Above ground
**APE WHEN FORMED**
va flow
**RAIN SIZE**  Fine
**OLOUR**  Grey, brown, green
**NERAL CONTENT**  Glassy,
ystalline fragments

## Syenite

Syenite is an attractive, multi-coloured rock, which may be polished and used as a decorative stone. It forms large crystals as it cools slowly underground. It looks similar to granite but unlike granite, it contains little, if any, quartz.

| | |
|---|---|
| **WHERE FORMED** | Below ground |
| **SHAPE WHEN FORMED** | Pluton, dyke, sill |
| **GRAIN SIZE** | Medium to coarse |
| **COLOUR** | Grey, pink, red |
| **MINERAL CONTENT** | Potassium feldspar, plagioclase, biotite, amphibole, pyroxene, feldspathoids |

## Dacite

Dacite derives its name from Dacia, a territory in the Roman Empire where it was first described. It forms part of several volcanoes, such as the one at Crater Lake, Oregon, USA.

| | |
|---|---|
| **WHERE FORMED** | Above ground |
| **SHAPE WHEN FORMED** | Pluton, dyke, sill |
| **GRAIN SIZE** | Fine |
| **COLOUR** | Grey to black |
| **MINERAL CONTENT** | Plagioclase, quartz, pyroxene, amphibole, biotite |

## Anorthosite

The ancient light-coloured highlands on the far side of the Moon are made of anorthosite. It forms large masses or layers between rocks such as gabbro and peridotite.

| | |
|---|---|
| **WHERE FORMED** | Below ground |
| **SHAPE WHEN FORMED** | Lava flow |
| **GRAIN SIZE** | Medium to coarse |
| **COLOUR** | Light grey to white |
| **MINERAL CONTENT** | Plagioclase, olivine, pyroxene, magnetite |

## rachyte

e name "trachyte" comes from the
reek word for "rough". This tough and
sistant rock has been used for paving
ads for thousands of years.

**HERE FORMED**  Above ground

**HAPE WHEN FORMED**  Lava flow, dyke, sill

**RAIN SIZE**  Fine to medium

**OLOUR**  Off-white, grey, pale yellow, pink

**INERAL CONTENT**
anidine, plagioclase,
dspathoids, quartz,
vine, pyroxene, biotite

## homb porphyry

rphyry refers to
neous rocks with
rge-grained
ystals. Rhomb
rphyry gets its
me from the
ombic, or
amond, shape
its large crystals.

**HERE FORMED**  Above ground

**HAPE WHEN FORMED**  Lava flow, dyke, sill

**RAIN SIZE**  Medium

**OLOUR**  Grey-white, red-brown, purple

**INERAL CONTENT**  Feldspar

## Pegmatite

Pegmatite is one of the sources of
important ore minerals, which provide
useful metals such as tungsten. Pegmatites
are also important sources of some gemstones,
and mica.

**WHERE FORMED**  Below ground

**SHAPE WHEN FORMED**  Pluton

**GRAIN SIZE**  Very coarse

**COLOUR**  Pink, white, cream

**MINERAL CONTENT**  Quartz, feldspar, mica,
tourmaline, topaz

The Devil's Tower is **sacred** to many Native American Plain tribes, who call it "Bear's Tip

**DEVIL'S TOWER**
The Devil's Tower in Wyoming, USA, is a giant structure of phonolite, an igneous rock. It formed when a volcano erupted and the magma cooled and solidified to form underground columns. Over millions of years, its surrounding layers weathered away, leaving the columns exposed.

# Sedimentary rocks

Sedimentary rocks make up 80–90 per cent of the rocks on Earth's surface. These rocks form on land when sediment or grains join together. They may be carried by wind or water to the sea where they are buried and form layers of rock.

▲ Chalk was used to make the first white colouring for art.

▲ Clay was often used by early artists for extracting the colour brown.

## Limestone

Fine texture

Fossil of shell

Limestone forms in warm, shallow seas and is made of the mineral calcite, which comes from sea water or the shells and skeletons of sea animals. It is used as a building stone and as a raw material in manufacturing glass. On burning it produces lime, which is used to make cement.

| | |
|---|---|
| **ORIGIN** | Sea bed |
| **GRAIN SIZE** | Fine to medium, angular to rounded |
| **COLOUR** | White, grey, pink |
| **MINERAL CONTENT** | Calcite |
| **FOSSILS** | Marine and freshwater invertebrates, plants |

## ock gypsum

o known as gyprock,
k gypsum forms when
er evaporates from
ans or salty lakes.
used as a
ilizer and
make
ster board.

**IGIN** Sea bed
**AIN SIZE**
dium to fine
stalline
**LOUR** White, pinkish, yellowish, grey
**NERAL CONTENT** Gypsum
**SSILS** None

## Dolomite

Dolomite rock is formed entirely of the
mineral dolomite. The Swiss Alps in Italy,
also known as the Dolomites, are almost
entirely composed of this rock.

Compact
carbonate
rock

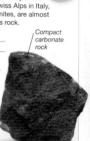

**ORIGIN** Land
**GRAIN SIZE** Fine to
medium, crystalline
**COLOUR** Grey to
yellowish-grey
**MINERAL CONTENT**
Dolomite
**FOSSILS**
Invertebrates

## ock salt

k salt forms when
y water evaporates.
well as being used in
hens as table salt, it is
d to make soaps and
king soda, among
er things.

**IGIN** Sea bed
**AIN SIZE** Coarse to fine crystalline
**LOUR** White, orange-brown, blue
**NERAL CONTENT** Halite
**SSILS** None

## Chalk

Chalk is made up of the mineral
calcite, which comes from the shells and
skeletons of sea animals. The grains in chalk
are so small that they cannot be seen without
a magnifying glass.

**ORIGIN** Sea bed
**GRAIN SIZE** Very fine,
angular to rounded
**COLOUR** White,
grey, buff
**MINERAL
CONTENT** Calcite
**FOSSILS**
Invertebrates,
vertebrates

## Peat

As plants decay over thousands of years, they slowly turn into coal. The formation of peat is the first step in this process. Peat forms in warm, moist climates, where there are enough nutrients, bacteria, and oxygen.

| | |
|---|---|
| **ORIGIN** | Land |
| **GRAIN SIZE** | Medium, fine |
| **COLOUR** | Dark brown to blac |
| **MINERAL CONTENT** | Carbon |
| **FOSSILS** | Plants, invertebrates |

## Anthracite

This form of coal contains a lot of carbon. It is glassy and cleaner to handle than other forms. Anthracite burns at a high temperature, with a blue flame, and produces very little smoke. It can be polished to make decorative items.

| | |
|---|---|
| **ORIGIN** | Land |
| **GRAIN SIZE** | Fine |
| **COLOUR** | Shiny black |
| **MINERAL CONTENT** | |
| Carbon | |
| **FOSSILS** | Plants |

# Travertine

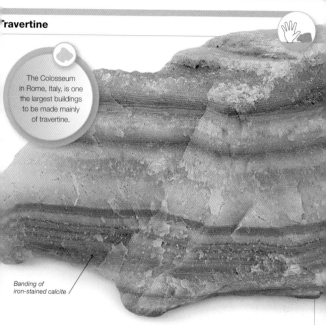

The Colosseum in Rome, Italy, is one the largest buildings to be made mainly of travertine.

Banding of iron-stained calcite

Travertine is usually found in caves, where forms stalagmites and stalactites. It may e formed by the evaporation of hot springs. he rock contains a pure form of calcium arbonate, and is often polished and used r walls and interior decorations.

| | |
|---|---|
| **ORIGIN** | Land |
| **GRAIN SIZE** | Crystalline |
| **COLOUR** | Creamy white |
| **MINERAL CONTENT** | Calcite |
| **FOSSILS** | Rare |

## Chert

This rock is so hard, it can't be scratched with a knife. In the Stone Age, it was used for making tools and weapons. Today, chert is used in building roads, and can even be polished to make jewellery.

**ORIGIN** Sea bed, or as nodules in limestone

**GRAIN SIZE** Fine, crystalline

**COLOUR** Greyish

**MINERAL CONTENT** Chalcedony

**FOSSILS** Invertebrates, plants

## Loess

The German word *loess* means "loose" and refers to the loose deposits of this rock by glacial winds. Loess is soft and crumbly and contains few clay minerals, so it feels smooth, not sticky, when wet.

**ORIGIN** Land

**GRAIN SIZE** Very fine

**COLOUR** Yellowish or brownish

**MINERAL CONTENT** Quartz, feldspar

**FOSSILS** Rare

## Tufa

Tufa is formed when lime-rich water evaporates leaving behind calcium carbonate. It gets deposited on cliffs, caves, and rock surfaces in regions where rainfall is low. In the process of formation, some pebbles and grains of sediment also get caught in it.

## Flint

In prehistoric times, people used flakes of flint to make sharp-edged weapons including knives, scrapers, and arrowheads. Flint is a hard substance, rich in silica, and it is found as bands in limestone.

| | |
|---|---|
| ORIGIN | Nodules in limestone or dolomite |
| GRAIN SIZE | Fine, crystalline |
| COLOUR | Grey |
| MINERAL CONTENT | Chalcedony |
| FOSSILS | Invertebrates |

Tufa towers form underwater and can reach heights of more than 9 m (30 ft).

## Feldspathic gritstone

This rock is made up of sand-sized grains and gravel. Iron oxides may help bind the grains together.

Feldspar grain

| | |
|---|---|
| ORIGIN | Sea bed, land |
| GRAIN SIZE | Coarse to medium, angular |
| COLOUR | Brownish with a tinge of pink |
| MINERAL CONTENT | Quartz, feldspar, mica |
| FOSSILS | Invertebrates, vertebrates, plants |

| | |
|---|---|
| **RIGIN** | Land |
| **RAIN SIZE** | Fine, crystalline |
| **LOUR** | White or orange-stained |
| **NERAL CONTENT** | Calcite or silica |
| **SSILS** | Rare |

## Shale

Shale is a highly fissile rock, meaning it breaks up into thin sheets. It forms from fine muds in various environments. Some shales have important deposits of oil in them.

**ORIGIN**  Sea bed, freshwater, glacier

**GRAIN SIZE**  Fine

**COLOUR**  Grey

**MINERAL CONTENT** Clays, quartz, calcite

**FOSSILS**  Invertebrates, vertebrates, plants

## Breccia

## Sandstone

Gaps between grains form different textures

Sandstones are classified by their different textures, which form from the way the sand-sized grains are cemented together. It is used as a building stone as it is durable.

**ORIGIN**  Land

**GRAIN SIZE**  Fine to medium, angular to rounded

**COLOUR**  Cream to red

**MINERAL CONTENT** Quartz, feldspar

**FOSSILS**  Vertebrates, invertebrates, plants

Breccia is a rock made up of generally large, rough grains cemented together. The lack of rounded grains shows that the rocks have not been transported far.

| | |
|---|---|
| **ORIGIN** | Sea bed, freshwater, glacier |
| **GRAIN SIZE** | Very coarse, angular |
| **COLOUR** | Varies |
| **MINERAL CONTENT** | Any hard mineral can be present |
| **FOSSILS** | Very rare |

## Conglomerate

Rocks that lie in water for a very long time become smooth and rounded. When these rocks are held together by cement, they form a conglomerate and may get transported long distances. Pebbles are the small rocks; cobbles are medium-sized rocks; and boulders are large. All these are larger than 2 mm (0.8 in) in size.

| | |
|---|---|
| **ORIGIN** | Sea bed, freshwater, glacier |
| **GRAIN SIZE** | Very coarse, rounded |
| **COLOUR** | Varies |
| **MINERAL CONTENT** | Any hard mineral can be present |
| **FOSSILS** | Very rare |

## rkose

This granitelike form of sandstone is different from other sandstones as it has more feldspar. It has a rough texture and its grains are usually cemented together by calcite.

| | |
|---|---|
| **RIGIN** | Sea bed, freshwater |
| **RAIN SIZE** | Medium, angular |
| **LOUR** | Pinkish to pale grey |
| **NERAL CONTENT** | Quartz, feldspar |
| **SSILS** | Rare |

## Ironstone

Sandstones and limestones with more than 15 per cent iron content are called ironstones. These ancient rocks formed when there was not as much oxygen in the atmosphere as today.

**ORIGIN** Sea bed or land

**GRAIN SIZE** Fine to medium, crystalline to angular, oolitic

**COLOUR** Red, black, grey, striped

**MINERAL CONTENT** Hematite, goethite, chamosite, magnetite, siderite, limonite, jasper

**FOSSILS** Invertebrates

## Clay

Clay grains are so fine that they can't even be seen with a microscope. Damp clay feels sticky, but adding water can make it flexible so it can be moulded into different form and shapes from pots and bricks to ornament

**ORIGIN** Sea bed, freshwater, land

**GRAIN SIZE** Fine

**COLOUR** Dark to light grey, white

**MINERAL CONTENT** Clay minerals, such as kaolinite, illite, montmorillonite

**FOSSILS** Plants, invertebrates, vertebrates

## Micaceous sandstone

This sandstone contains a high quantity of mica minerals. The mica appears as small flakes in t rock, which are very light and easily blown away in sediments deposited on land. This shows that it's more likely to have been deposited in wat

**ORIGIN** Sea bed or freshwater

**GRAIN SIZE** Medium, angular to flattened

**COLOUR** Buff, green, grey, pink

**MINERAL CONTENT** Quartz, feldspar, mica

**FOSSILS** Invertebrates, plants, vertebrates

# Septarian nodule

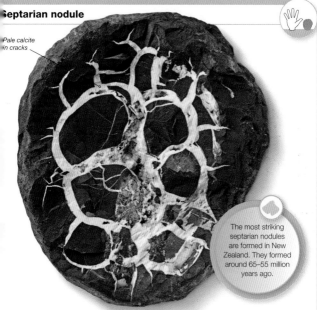

Pale calcite in cracks

The most striking septarian nodules are formed in New Zealand. They formed around 65–55 million years ago.

Nodules and concretions are features that develop after a sedimentary rock forms. Concretions are made of the same minerals as the host rock, but nodules have a different mineral content. Septarian nodules are harder than the surrounding rock. They form when a nodule shrinks and cracks. The cracks fill up with light-coloured minerals such as calcite.

**ORIGIN** Sea bed, land

**GRAIN SIZE** Fine to medium, angular to rounded

**COLOUR** Cream to red

**MINERAL CONTENT** Calcite or celestine

**FOSSILS** Vertebrates, invertebrates, plants

# The Wave is made of
# 190 million-year-old
## sand dunes that have
## turned to rock

**THE WAVE**
The Wave, in Arizona, USA, is a natural formation of sandstone rocks that look like a cresting ocean wave. The different layers have been formed by wind deposition. The rocks' varied colours are caused by the presence of different minerals, including hematite.

# Metamorphic rocks

When pressure and temperature act upo
existing rocks, the atoms and minerals
rearrange to form new rocks. These are
called metamorphic rocks.

## Phyllite

Wavy foliat

Phyllite is a dark coloured rock with an irregular
surface. The large grains of mica in it make it shiny.
It is sometimes used for making pavements.

| | |
|---|---|
| **ORIGINAL ROCK** | Mudstone, shale |
| **HOW FORMED** | Regional change |
| **TEMPERATURE** | Low to moderate |
| **PRESSURE** | Low |
| **COLOUR** | Silvery to greenish-grey |

## arble

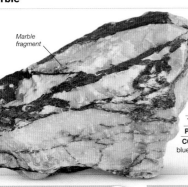

Marble fragment

Pure marble is white. Impurities can make it multi-coloured. Some marbles, such as pink and green marble, take their common names from their colour or mineral impurities.

**ORIGINAL ROCK** Limestone

**HOW FORMED** Regional change, thermal contact

**TEMPERATURE** High

**PRESSURE** Low to high

**COLOUR** White, pink, green, blue, grey

## ate

Slate is an important roofing material and was also used to make chalkboards. It is quarried in large pieces, for use in electrical panels. Plant and animal fossils can be preserved in slate.

**IGINAL ROCK** Clay, mudstones, shale, tuff

**W FORMED** Regional change

**MPERATURE** Low

**ESSURE** Low

**LOUR** Grey, purple, green

## Schist

Schist rock has visible mineral grains in it. It is rich in micas or chlorite, and splits easily along crinkly surfaces.

**ORIGINAL ROCK** Mud- and clay-based rocks

**HOW FORMED** Regional change

**TEMPERATURE** Low to moderate

**PRESSURE** Low to moderate

**COLOUR** Silvery, green

## Hornfels

This rock forms at temperatures as high as 800°C (1,472°F). There are many varieties depending on the minerals in the rock. Hornfels rock is hard to break.

Hornblende and plagioclase

| | |
|---|---|
| **ORIGINAL ROCK** | Almost any rock |
| **HOW FORMED** | Thermal contact |
| **TEMPERATURE** | Moderate to high |
| **PRESSURE** | Low to high |
| **COLOUR** | Dark grey, brown, greenish, reddish |

## Amphibolite

Roads are often built using amphibolite to give them strength and durability. This rock is also used as an ornamental stone.

| | |
|---|---|
| **ORIGINAL ROCK** | Basalt greywacke, dolomite |
| **HOW FORMED** | Regional change |
| **TEMPERATURE** | Low to moderate |
| **PRESSURE** | Low to moderate |
| **COLOUR** | Grey, black, greenish |

## Quartzite

Quartzite is formed when sandstones are buried, heated, and squeezed. Quartzite is made up of 90 per cent quartz. It is quarried for use as raw material for building roads, laying roofs, and paving blocks.

# Fulgurite

The word fulgurite comes from the Latin *fulgur*, meaning "thunderbolt". This rock forms when lightning strikes sand. Lightning in deserts tends to melt the sand, which then fuses into a fulgurite, forming tubes and crusts.

| | |
|---|---|
| **ORIGINAL ROCK** | Usually sand |
| **HOW FORMED** | Thermal contact |
| **TEMPERATURE** | Very high |
| **PRESSURE** | Low |
| **COLOUR** | Grey, white, black |

| | |
|---|---|
| **ORIGINAL ROCK** | Sandstone |
| **HOW FORMED** | Regional change |
| **TEMPERATURE** | High |
| **PRESSURE** | Low to high |
| **COLOUR** | White, pink |

# Skarn

Skarn is rich in carbonate, calcium, iron, and magnesium silicates. These form different-coloured patches in the rock. Some skarn minerals are rich sources of metals and can be valuable deposits of gold, copper, iron, tin, and zinc.

**ORIGINAL ROCK**
Limestone, dolomite

**HOW FORMED**
Thermal contact

**TEMPERATURE**  High

**PRESSURE**  Low

**COLOUR**  Brown

*Typical veined and banded structure*

*Dark minera bands*

# Migmatite

Migmatite means "mixed rock". It consists of gneiss or schists mixed with granite. The granite melts slightly, forming streaks that are lighter in colour than the dark bands of gneiss or schists.

**ORIGINAL ROCK** Various, including granite and gneiss

**HOW FORMED** Regional change

**TEMPERATURE** High

**PRESSURE** High

**COLOUR** Banded light and dark grey, pink, white

# Serpentinite

This rock is the state rock of California, USA. It forms deep within Earth's crust where tectonic plates meet. Made up of serpentine minerals, this rock is known for its marblelike look and feel.

**ORIGINAL ROCK** Peridotite

**HOW FORMED** Regional change

**TEMPERATURE** Low

**PRESSURE** High

**COLOUR** Mottled green

## Gneiss

This rock is usually found buried deep in mountain-building regions that experience great heat and pressure. As it does not split easily, gneiss is used as a building material for flooring and facing stones. It is also used as an ornamental stone for worktops and even gravestones.

| | |
|---|---|
| **ORIGINAL ROCK** | Granite, shale, granodiorite, mudstone, siltstone, or felsic volcanics |
| **HOW FORMED** | Regional change |
| **TEMPERATURE** | High |
| **PRESSURE** | High |
| **COLOUR** | Grey, pink, multi-coloured |

## Mylonite

Mylonite is a crushed rock. It forms on fault planes when movements in Earth's crust exert great pressure but little heat. The pressure exerted on the rock gives it a wavy texture.

| | |
|---|---|
| **ORIGINAL ROCK** | Varies |
| **HOW FORMED** | Dynamic press |
| **TEMPERATURE** | Low |
| **PRESSURE** | High |
| **COLOUR** | Dark or light |

## clogite

Found in the uppermost part of Earth's mantle, eclogite forms at very high temperatures and pressures. It is a coarse-grained rock that is made up of two main minerals – green omphacite pyroxene and red garnet – and often quartz too.

| | |
|---|---|
| **ORIGINAL ROCK** | Igneous rocks |
| **HOW FORMED** | Regional change |
| **TEMPERATURE** | High |
| **PRESSURE** | High |
| **COLOUR** | Pale green, red |

**Gneiss is named either from the old German word for spark or the old Saxon word for**

# decayed and rotten

**BANDED GNEISS**
This gneiss rock has been eroded and polished by river water rushing past. This reveals the bands of different minerals that separated and folded into layers as the rock formed. Gneiss forms under very high temperature and pressure.

# Meteorites

When parts of rocky asteroids and comets break off in space and fall to Earth, they are called meteorites. As they come from space, they are not classified as igneous, sedimentary, or metamorphic.

**FOCUS ON...
CRATERS**
When a meteorite lands on Earth, it can cause a large impact crater.

## Achondrites

Stony meteorites are classified as chondrites and achondrites. The latter are those that do not contain chondrules – miniature igneous rocks that formed in space. Achondrites resemble the rocks found in Earth's mantle and crust.

| | |
|---|---|
| **ORIGIN** | Space |
| **GRAIN SIZE** | Medium to coarse |
| **COLOUR** | Black, grey, yellow |
| **MINERAL CONTENT** | Pyroxene, olivine, plagioclase feldspar |
| **FOSSILS** | None |

## Tektite

When large meteorites hit Earth, they can melt rocks on our planet, which can get thrown in the air and quickly cool to form glassy objects are called tektites, from the Greek word for "melted".

| | |
|---|---|
| **ORIGIN** | Meteorite impact |
| **GRAIN SIZE** | Crystalline |
| **COLOUR** | Green, black |
| **MINERAL CONTENT** | Silicate |
| **FOSSILS** | None |

he 168-m- (550-ft-) deep Barringer Meteorite ter in Arizona, USA, is one of the best known act craters on Earth.

▲ The circular Lac à l'Eau Claire, or the Clearwater Lakes, in Quebec, Canada, were formed by meteorite impacts around 210 million years ago.

## tony-iron meteorites

hese are mixtures of iron and silicate inerals. Stony-iron meteorites help ientists understand planets such as ars, which has iron and silicate materials.

| | |
|---|---|
| **RIGIN** | Space |
| **RAIN SIZE** | Fine to medium |
| **OLOUR** | Grey, greenish, tan, or black |
| **INERAL CONTENT** | Olivine, yroxene, plagioclase |
| **OSSILS** | None |

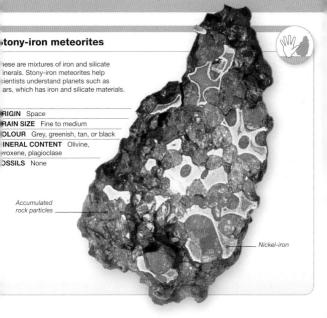

*Accumulated rock particles*

*Nickel-iron*

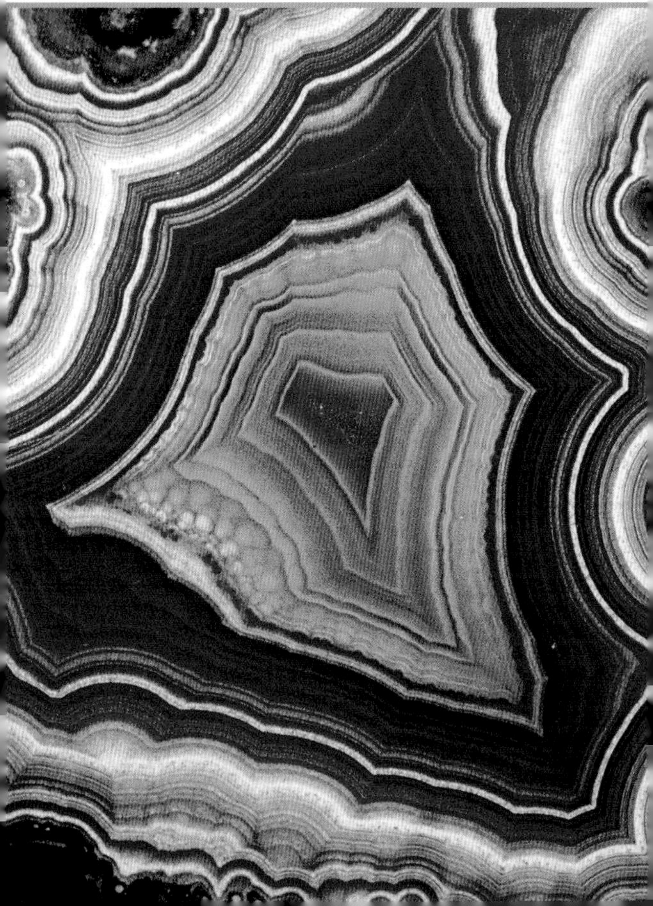

# Minerals

Minerals are all around us. There are more than 4,500 known minerals, but only 100 of these are common. They are naturally occurring solids that are made up of particular combinations of chemicals. Minerals make up much of our planet and provide many things we use every day, from copper pipes to jewellery to toothpaste.

**MALACHITE BOX**
This malachite jewel box was made in 1989. Polished malachite is a popular decorative material for buildings and ornaments.

# Where minerals form

Minerals form in many different environments – in rocks, in the sea, inside Earth, and even in human bones. The way they grow may be affected by temperature and pressure. Some minerals take thousan of years to develop, while others grow in only a few hours.

## Sedimentary minerals

Minerals can form on Earth's surface. When hot, mineral-rich, salty water evaporates, the minerals left behind are known as evaporites. Calcite, which forms limestone rocks, also develops in sea water.

Wulfenite deposits in cracks of lead ore

## Mineral veins

Water found in hot springs and beneath volcanoes often carries dissolved minerals. These are deposited in cracks and cavities of rocks forming mineral veins

Calcite deposits are found at Mammoth Hot Springs in Yellowstone National Park, USA

Olivine is found in igneous rocks

## Metamorphic minerals

In mountain-forming areas, heat and pressure change existing rocks, and new minerals grow. These metamorphic minerals usually have a good crystal shape. Some minerals, such as garnet, form over hundreds of thousands of years as heat and pressure gradually alter the rocks.

**neous minerals**

jma inside Earth contains chemicals are present in minerals. The minerals elop when magma and lava begin to I and solidify to form igneous rocks.

The mineral spinel grows when metamorphic rocks change

# Mineral groups

There are thousands of minerals on Earth.
These have been divided into 12 main groups,
or families, based on the chemicals they contain.
While some minerals are abundant,
others – including diamonds – are
very rare and highly prized.

Gold in
quartz

## Native elements

Most minerals are made from
combinations of chemical elements, but
a few elements, such as silver, gold, and
sulphur, occur naturally by themselves.
These are known as native elements.

## Sulphides

Sulphur combines with metals to form
sulphides. They form near geothermal
springs or in veins with
quartz. Sulphides include
cinnabar and pyrite.

Cinnabar is
a mercury
sulphide

## Sulphosalts

This a group of 200 rare minerals that
form when sulphur combines with a
metal (silver, copper, lead, or iron) and
a semi-metal (arsenic or antimony).

Proustite
contains
arsenic

## Oxides

Oxides form when oxygen combines with metals. They include ores (minerals from which metals are extracted) and gems.

**Rutile** forms when titanium and oxygen combine

## Hydroxides

These minerals form when a metallic element combines with hydrogen and oxygen. These minerals are less dense than oxides and tend to be softer. Hydroxides are also important ore minerals. They include bauxite, which is an ore of aluminium.

**Bauxite**

## Halides

In these soft minerals, metals combine with chlorine, bromine, fluorine, or iodine. For example, sylvite is a combination of potassium and chlorine.

Glassy, cube-shaped **crystals**

**Sylvite**

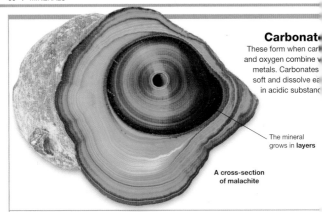

## Carbonate

These form when car[bon]
and oxygen combine w[ith]
metals. Carbonates [are]
soft and dissolve ea[sily]
in acidic substan[ces]

The mineral
grows in **layers**

A cross-section
of malachite

Erythrite is
an arsenate

## Phosphates, arsenates,
## and vanadates

These rare minerals are grouped together
because they have a similar structure, made up
of oxygen combined with phosphorus, arsenic, or
vanadium. They often have vivid colours.

## Borates and nitrates

Borates form when a metallic element
combines with boron and oxygen. Wh[en]
nitrogen and oxygen combine with a
metallic element, nitrates are formed.

Glassy lustre

Boracite
crystals

alcanthite
sulphate

## Sulphates, chromates, molybdates, tungstates

Around 200 minerals make up this large group. They share a similar structure and elements – oxygen combined with a metal or semi-metal. These minerals are dense, brittle, and may be vividly coloured.

## Silicates

This group makes up a quarter of all known minerals. As well as being common, silicates such as feldspar and quartz are important rock-forming minerals. Other silicates include mica, garnet, and natrolite. All silicates contain silicon and oxygen.

**Natrolite**

## Organic minerals

These are a group of minerals that form from living things, and may or may not have a crystal structure. Amber, coral, and pearl are organic gems. Amber forms from the resin of conifer trees, coral from sea creatures, and pearl comes from certain shellfish and oysters.

**Red coral**

# Identifying minerals

There are many ways to identify a mineral, including observing its colour and shape, and how it looks when light reflects off it. The hardness of a mineral can be measured by how easily it scratches.

## Crystal systems

Minerals have different "crystal systems", or crystal shapes. There are six groups:

| Cubic | Monoclinic | Triclinic | Trigonal/ hexagonal | Orthorhombic | Tetragon |

## Cleavage

Cleavage describes how easily and cleanly a mineral breaks along its natural weak points. Perfect cleavage produces a smooth, shiny surface. Cleavage can also be difficult, distinct, or "none" (leaving rough, uneven surfaces).

**Obsidian**
fractures w
a conchoid
or shell-like
pattern

**Iceland spar,**
a type of calcite, cleaves to make a perfect rhombic shape

## Fracture

This is how cleanly a mineral breaks in places other than its cleavage lines. Fract can leave jagged edges (hackly), rough but flat surfaces (even), shell-like scoops (conchoidal), or no pattern at all (uneven).

## bit

neral's habit, or general shape,
nds on the pattern that its crystals
as they grow. If there is no clear
e, it is called "massive".

**lecite** looks
needles

**Copper** has a
plantlike shape

**Actinolite** looks
like knife blades

**Beryl looks** like
a prism with a
regular shape

# Hardness

Mohs' scale, invented by the mineralogist Friedrich Mohs, meas[ures] how hard a mineral is based on ho[w] easily it scratches. The scale cons[ists] of 10 minerals arranged from 1 to [10]. The higher the number, the harder [the] mineral. Every mineral can scratch [the] ones listed below it and get scratch[ed] by minerals above it on the scale.

**Finger nail: 2.5**

## MOHS' SCALE OF HARDNESS

**1: Talc**

**2: Gypsum**

**3: Calcite**

**4: Fluorite**

**5: Apatite**

**6: Orthoclase**

**7: Quartz**

**8: Topaz**

**9: Corundum**

**10: Diamo[nd]**

# Specific gravity (SG)

This is a measure of how heavy a mineral is compared to an equal volume of water.

**The SG** of jasper is 2.7, meaning it is 2.7 times heavier than water.

# Colour

Some minerals come in more than one co[lour]. Usually this is because the mineral conta[ins] impurities or its crystals are flawed.

**Fluorite** is known for its many different colours.

## treak

a mineral is crushed
into a powder and
awn on porcelain, it
oduces a streak. The
lour of the streak may
t be the same as the
neral colour.

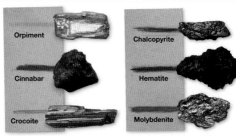

Orpiment

Cinnabar

Crocoite

Chalcopyrite

Hematite

Molybdenite

## Transparency

If light can pass through a mineral, it is
called translucent. If a mineral is opaque,
no light can pass through it. Transparent
minerals are clear and see-through.

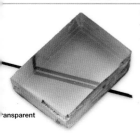

ansparent

Translucent

Opaque

## ustre

is describes how shiny
mineral is when sunlight
lects off it. Lustres
clude dull, greasy, silky,
etallic, waxy, and vitreous
assy). The shiniest is
amantine (diamondlike).

Galena looks like metal when
light reflects off it

Quartz has
a glasslike,
or vitreous,
lustre

Metallic

Vitreous

# Gemstones

Some minerals are brilliantly coloured and form striking and large crystals that are used as gemstones. They are valued for their beauty and rarity – there's nothing chemical that makes gemstones different from other minerals. More than 4,500 minerals exist, but only 100 are used as gemstones.

Gemstones often look **dull** before they are cut and polished

**Uncut Burmese ruby crystal**

## Cutting and polishing

To bring out the beauty of gemstones, they are cut and polished. Coloured stones, such as rubies, are cut in different ways to bring out the rich colours. Opaque or translucent stones are generally cut into a smooth oval. Some gems may be beautiful but too soft or brittle to be cut and worn.

**Different cuts** bring out the beauty of a gemstone

**Mixed cut ruby**

**Brilliant cut aquamarine**

**Step cut zircon**

# Precious gems

There are two kinds of gem: precious and semi-precious. Only seven gemstones – diamond, aquamarine, emerald, sapphire, ruby, topaz, and opal – are regarded as precious. Jewellers use different gemstone cuts, colours, and combinations to make dazzling pieces of jewellery.

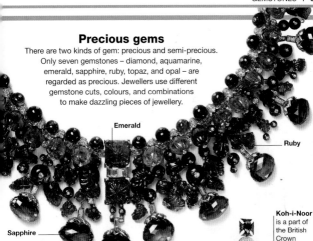

**Emerald**

**Ruby**

**Sapphire**

**Koh-i-Noor** is a part of the British Crown Jewels

# Organic gems

Most gems come from rocks, but some have an organic origin, which means they come from living things. For example, pearls form in certain shellfish and oysters. Others include coral (from sea creatures), amber (from tree resin), and jet (from coal).

**Pearl on oyster shell**

# Megagems

Some gemstones stand out for their extraordinary beauty and size. These are called megagems. The Koh-i-Noor diamond weighs 109 carats (21.8 g/0.77 oz).

FOCUS ON...
**GOLD**
Apart from being
used in jewellery,
gold has many
other applications.

# Native elements

Chemical elements that occur in nature by themselves rather than with other elements are called native elements. They can be classified into three groups: metals, semi-metals, and non-metals.

▲ Worldwide, dentists use about 23 kg (50 lb) of gold a day for making tooth fillings.

▲ Many microchips in computers are made of gold circuits that allow data to flow in the computer.

▲ The plastic visor of an astronaut's spacesuit helmet is coated with gold to protect the astronaut from the Sun's glare.

## Copper

Native copper is found close to Earth's surface above other copper deposits. Copper in its natural state was probably the first metal used by people, who made it into weapons and tools as a substitute for stone. It is now used in electrical wires and deep-sea cables, among other things.

| HARDNESS 2.5–3 | SG 8.9 |
|---|---|
| COLOUR Copper-red to brown | |
| TRANSPARENCY Opaque | |
| LUSTRE Metallic | |

## atinum

atinum is rarer than gold. As well as
ng used in jewellery, it is also used to
ne fuel to reduce pollution from cars.

| **ARDNESS** 4–4.5 | **SG** 14–19 |
| --- | --- |
| **OLOUR** Whitish steel-grey | |
| **ANSPARENCY** Opaque | |
| **STRE** Metallic | |

## Gold

Gold has been a measure of wealth since
ancient times. It is ideal for making jewellery
because it is soft and can be easily worked
into different shapes. Jewellers sometimes
mix it with metals such as silver and copper to
make it harder. Gold is also valued because it
does not lose its colour or lustre when exposed
to air. South Africa is the largest producer of
gold in the world.

| **HARDNESS** 2.5–3 | **SG** 19.3 |
| --- | --- |
| **COLOUR** Golden-yellow | |
| **TRANSPARENCY** Opaque | |
| **LUSTRE** Metallic | |

## ilver

strong conductor of electricity and
at, silver is widely used in the electrical
ustry. It is a popular raw material in the
aking of jewellery and coins. The leading
oducer of silver is Peru.

| **ARDNESS** 2.5–3 | **SG** 10.1–11.1 |
| --- | --- |
| **OLOUR** Silver-white | |
| **ANSPARENCY** aque | |
| **STRE** etallic | |

# Sulphur

The ancient Chinese discovered how to make gunpowder from sulphur.

Sulphur forms around hot springs and volcanic craters. It burns with a blue flame if held over a lighted match. Mined on a large scale, sulphur is widely used in explosives, fertilizers, dyes, drugs, and detergents.

| | |
|---|---|
| **HARDNESS** | 1.5–2.5 |
| **SG** | 2.1 |
| **COLOUR** | Yellow |
| **TRANSPARENCY** | Transparent to translucent |
| **LUSTRE** | Resinous to greasy |

# Diamond

A pure form of carbon, diamond is the hardest mineral on Earth. Diamond-tipped drills and saws can cut through any substance. The glittery brilliance of diamond makes it the most valuable gemstone in the world.

| | |
|---|---|
| **HARDNESS** 10 | **SG** 3.4–3.5 |

**COLOUR** White to black, colourless, yellow, pink, red, blue, brown

**TRANSPARENCY** Transparent to opaque

**LUSTRE** Diamondlike

# Graphite

This mineral takes its name from the Greek word *graphein*, which means "to write". It leaves a black mark when rubbed on paper and is used in pencils. It is also one of the softest minerals and can be cut with a knife.

| | |
|---|---|
| **HARDNESS** | 1–2 |
| **SG** | 2.2 |
| **COLOUR** | Black |
| **TRANSPARENCY** | Opaque |
| **LUSTRE** | Metallic or dull earthy |

# Iron

Iron makes up 5 per cent of Earth's crust. After oxygen, silicon, and aluminium, it is the fourth most abundant chemical in the crust. It is used to make a vast number of things, including steel, magnets, and car parts.

| | |
|---|---|
| **HARDNESS** 4.5 | **SG** 7.3–7.9 |

**COLOUR** Steel-grey to iron-black

**TRANSPARENCY** Opaque

**LUSTRE** Metallic

## Nickel-iron

Often found in meteorites on Earth's surface, nickel-iron used to be called "sky-iron" by the ancient Egyptians. They used it to make sacred tools for mummifying pharaohs.

| | | | |
|---|---|---|---|
| **HARDNESS** 4-5 | | **SG** 7.3-8.2 | |
| **COLOUR** Steel-grey, dark grey, blackish | | | |
| **TRANSPARENCY** Opaque | | | |
| **LUSTRE** Metallic | | | |

## Bismuth

This rare native element is mostly found in hydrothermal veins and pegmatites. It is a semi-metal – it expands on freezing, just as water expands when it turns into ice.

**HARDNESS** 2–2.5

**SG** 9.7–9.8

**COLOUR** Silver-white with reddish tarnish

**TRANSPARENCY** Opaque

**LUSTRE** Metallic

## Arsenic

When heated, this mineral quickly turns into gas without melting. Though poisonous, it was used in some medicines to treat infections. Arsenic was also used to make pesticides.

**HARDNESS** 3.5

**SG** 5.7

**COLOUR** Tin-white

**TRANSPARENCY** Opaque

**LUSTRE** Metallic or dull earthy

## ercury

ive mercury exists in a poisonous, liquid
n at room temperature. It is used in
rmometers because even a minor change in
perature can cause it to expand or contract.

| HARDNESS Liquid | SG 13.6–14.4 |
| --- | --- |
| COLOUR Silver-white | |
| TRANSPARENCY Opaque | |
| LUSTRE Metallic | |

Mercury was
named after the
Roman god
of trade.

# e **deepest** point in the

# nakil desert is 100 m (328 ft) below sea level

**SULPHUR**
Earth's lowest lying desert, the Danakil in Ethiopia, is known for its extreme heat. It is made up of volcanoes, hot springs, and acidic ponds. Bright yellow sulphur crystallizes around volcanic craters, adding beautiful shapes and colour to the landscape.

**FOCUS ON...**
## USES
Chemical elements obtained from sulphides have many different uses.

▲ The blue colour in fireworks comes from stibnite, which is a source of antimony.

▲ Roman ingots are made of lead, which is extracted from galena and other lead sulphides.

◄ Cinnabar contains mercury, which is used in thermometers.

# Sulphides

In these minerals, sulphur combines with one or more metals. They have a metallic lustre and can conduct electricity, but not as well as metals. They are important sources of lead, zinc, iron, and copper and a good source of silver and platinum.

### Galena

A valuable mineral since Roman times, galena is the principle ore of lead. It develops mineral-rich cubic crystals, which form when hot fluids find their way to higher levels in Earth's crust.

| | |
|---|---|
| **HARDNESS** | 2.5 |
| **SG** | 7.6 |
| **COLOUR** | Lead-grey |
| **TRANSPARENCY** | Opaque |
| **LUSTRE** | Metallic |

# Sphalerite

Sphalerite can occur in several different forms and is often mistaken for galena. This sulphide is an important source of zinc and can also be used as a gemstone.

**HARDNESS** 3–4

**SG** 3.9–4.1

**COLOUR** Brown, black, yellow

**TRANSPARENCY** Opaque to transparent

**LUSTRE** Resinous to diamondlike, metallic

# Acanthite

Occurring as spiky crystals, acanthite takes its name from the Greek word *akantha*, meaning "thorn". This sulphide is the main source of silver.

**HARDNESS** 2–2.5          **SG** 7.2–7.4

**COLOUR** Black

**TRANSPARENCY** Opaque

**LUSTRE** Metallic

# Bornite

Known as "peacock ore" because of its iridescent splash of colours, bornite is a source of copper. Bornite crystals are rarely found as it usually occurs as massive aggregates.

**HARDNESS** 3          **SG** 5.1

**COLOUR** Coppery red, brown

**TRANSPARENCY** Opaque

**LUSTRE** Metallic

## Covellite

This sulphide of copper is named after the Italian Nicolas Covelli, who first described it. It was first collected and identified at Mount Vesuvius, near Naples, Italy. When heated, covellite produces a blue-coloured flame.

| | |
|---|---|
| **HARDNESS** | 1.5–2 |
| **SG** | 4.6–4.7 |
| **COLOUR** | Indigo-blue to black |
| **TRANSPARENCY** | Opaque |
| **LUSTRE** | Submetallic to resinous |

## Pentlandite

Named after Irish scientist Joseph Pentland, pentlandite is a major ore of nickel. Nickel ores need extensive refining for releasing the metal. Deposits have been found in Canada and Russia, and also in meteorites.

| | |
|---|---|
| **HARDNESS** | 3.5–4 |
| **SG** | 4.6–5 |
| **COLOUR** | Bronze-yellow |
| **TRANSPARENCY** | Opaque |
| **LUSTRE** | Metallic |

## Cinnabar

Highly poisonous, cinnabar is the main ore of mercury. It is the central ingredient in the pigment vermilion, and its brilliant orange-red colour was used in paintings in ancient China. Cinnabar often forms around volcanic vents and hot springs.

| | | | |
|---|---|---|---|
| **HARDNESS** | 2–2.5 | **SG** | 8 |
| **COLOUR** | Red | | |
| **TRANSPARENCY** | Transparent to opaque | | |
| **LUSTRE** | Diamondlike to dull | | |

## reenockite

s mineral is a cadmium ore, which
sed for plating steel and other metals
t get corroded easily. It is mixed with
kel to make rechargeable batteries.

**RDNESS** 3–3.5   **SG** 4.8–4.9

**LOUR** Yellow, orange,
nge-yellow, red

**ANSPARENCY**
arly opaque
ranslucent

**STRE**
sinous or
mondlike

*Greenockite coating*

## Pyrrhotite

This magnetic mineral is a mixture of
iron and sulphur in varying amounts. The
amount of iron affects its magnetic properties.
The mineral name is derived from the Greek
word *pyrrhos*, which means "flame-coloured".

**HARDNESS** 3.5–4.5   **SG** 4.6–4.7

**COLOUR** Bronze-yellow to copper bronze-red

**TRANSPARENCY** Opaque

**LUSTRE** Metallic

# Realgar

After handling realgar, it's important to wash your hands because of the arsenic content.

Characterized by its bright red crystals, realgar has been used in Chinese art and for making fireworks. However, when exposed to light, the crystals crumble and form a yellow crust. Realgar is an important ore of the poison arsenic and is itself poisonous.

| HARDNESS 1.5–2 | SG 3.6 |
|---|---|
| COLOUR Scarlet to orange-yellow | |
| TRANSPARENCY Subtransparent to opaque | |
| LUSTRE Resinous to greasy | |

## halcocite

ne of the most important ores of
pper, chalcocite crystals were mined in
ornwall, England, for centuries. Copper is
ed for making aircraft, and other commercial
d domestic purposes.

| HARDNESS | 2.5–3 |
|---|---|
| SG | 5.5–5.8 |
| COLOUR | Blackish lead-grey |
| TRANSPARENCY | Opaque |
| LUSTRE | Metallic |

## Stannite

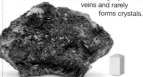

Stannite, an ore of tin, is found at
Zeehan in Tasmania, Australia, and Cornwall
in England. It occurs in tin-bearing, hydrothermal
veins and rarely
forms crystals.

| HARDNESS | 4 | SG | 4.4 |
|---|---|---|---|
| COLOUR | Steel-grey to iron-black | | |
| TRANSPARENCY | Opaque | | |
| LUSTRE | Metallic | | |

## halcopyrite

ough not very rich in copper,
widespread occurrence makes
alcopyrite an important copper
. It is commonly found in
drothermal ore veins deposited
high and medium temperatures.

| RDNESS | 3.5–4 |
|---|---|
| | 4.2 |
| LOUR | Brass-yellow |
| ANSPARENCY | Opaque |
| STRE | Metallic |

# Stibnite

Stibnite's long, prism-shaped crystals have an
unusual property – they can grow twisted and
bent. Stibnite is the main ore of antimony, which is
used for hardening lead and is added to paint and
plastics as a flame-retardant.

| HARDNESS | 2 | SG | 4.6 |
|---|---|---|---|
| COLOUR | Lead-grey to steel-grey, black | | |
| TRANSPARENCY | Opaque | | |
| LUSTRE | Metallic | | |

Prismlike
crystals

In ancient times,
powdered stibnite was
used as make-up to
darken eyelashes
and eyebrows.

# Millerite

This sulphide is an ore of nickel, used in metal alloys. It forms in needle-like crystals or in masses. It normally forms at low temperatures in holes in limestone or dolomite rocks, and is also found in meteorites. Millerite is named after English mineralogist W H Miller who first studied it.

*Calcite groundmass*

*Millerite crystal*

**HARDNESS** 3–3.5

**SG** 5.5

**COLOUR** Brass-yellow

**TRANSPARENCY** Opaque

**LUSTRE** Metallic

## Orpiment

Orpiment takes its name from the Latin *auri pigmentum*, meaning "golden paint". Pigment derived from it was used in 19th-century paintings. However, it contains arsenic, which is poisonous.

| | |
|---|---|
| **HARDNESS** 1.5–2 | **SG** 3.5 |

**COLOUR** Yellow

**TRANSPARENCY** Transparent to translucent

**LUSTRE** Resinous

## Pyrite

## Bismuthinite

This rare mineral is a source of bismuth. When bismuth is mixed with other metals, it has a low melting point and is used in fire-safety devices, such as sprinkler heads.

**HARDNESS** 2

**SG** 6.8

**COLOUR** Lead-grey to tin-white

**TRANSPARENCY** Opaque

**LUSTRE** Metallic

## Marcasite

In the late Victorian era, marcasite was used to make mourning jewellery, worn at funeral ceremonies and other sombre occasions. Its crystals tend to darken with exposure to air.

**HARDNESS** 6–6.5

**SG** 4.9

**COLOUR** Pale bronze-yellow

**TRANSPARENCY** Opaque

**LUSTRE** Metallic

*Chalk groundmass*

so called fool's gold, pyrite was often
[mi]staken for gold because of its brassy
[co]lour and high density. Pyrite gets its name
[fro]m Greek *pyr*, meaning "fire", as it emits
[sp]arks when struck by iron.

*Cubic habit*

**HARDNESS** 6–6.5

**SG** 5

**COLOUR** Pale brass-yellow

**TRANSPARENCY** Opaque

**LUSTRE** Metallic

## Hauerite

This manganese
sulphide occurs in areas
with salt deposits. It is
found in Texas, USA;
the Ural Mountains of
Russia; and Sicily, Italy.

**HARDNESS** 4

**SG** 3.5

**COLOUR** Red-brown to
brown-black

**TRANSPARENCY** Opaque

**LUSTRE** Diamondlike to
submetallic

## Cobaltite

Also known as cobalt glance,
cobaltite is a source of cobalt.
Cobalt is mixed with metals to
make machine parts stronger
and heat-resistant.

**HARDNESS** 5.5

**SG** 6.3

**COLOUR**
Silver-white, pink

**TRANSPARENCY**
Opaque

**LUSTRE**
Metallic

# Arsenopyrite

This mineral is found in metamorphic and igneous rocks, in ore veins that form at moderate to high temperatures. It is the main source of arsenic and the most common of the minerals that contain this poison.

**HARDNESS** 5.5–6   **SG** 6.1

**COLOUR** Silver-white to steel-grey

**TRANSPARENCY** Opaque

**LUSTRE** Metallic

*Crystals are marked with grooves*

When heated or struck, arsenopyrite gives off an odour that smells like garlic.

## Molybdenite

This sulphide was originally mistaken for lead and so its name came from the Greek word for lead, *molybdos*. When added to alloys, it increases the hardness of iron and steel, protecting them against corrosion.

| | |
|---|---|
| **HARDNESS** 1–1.5 | **SG** 4.7 |
| **COLOUR** Lead-grey | |
| **TRANSPARENCY** Opaque | |
| **LUSTRE** Metallic | |

## Sylvanite

Sylvanite is often found in small quantities in gold and silver deposits. It is photosensitive, which means it reacts to light, and can acquire a dark tarnish if exposed to bright light for too long.

| | |
|---|---|
| **HARDNESS** 1–2 | **SG** 8.2 |
| **COLOUR** Silver-white to pale yellow | |
| **TRANSPARENCY** Opaque | |
| **LUSTRE** Metallic | |

**COPPER**

Chalcocite is one of the most important sources of copper, which is the oldest metal known to man. Copper is mainly obtained by smelting and refining. Smelting usually involves heat and a chemical to extract copper from its ore.

**Copper was the first metal to be separated from its ore, probably around 10,000 years ago**

# Sulphosalts

Sulphosalts are a large group of mostly rare minerals in which sulphur combines with a metal and a non-metal. They have a lustre similar to that of a metal and are dense and brittle.

FOCUS ON...
## SITES
There are several sites across the world that are known for their sources of sulphosalts.

▲ The Giant Mountains in Czech Republic are a key site for polybasite and proustite.

▲ Jamesonite and tennantite are found in abundance in Chihuahua, Mexico.

▲ The Harz Mountains in Germany are a source of many sulphosalts, such as bournonite, boulangerite, and zinkenite.

## Tetrahedrite

Tetrahedrite is an important ore of copper and has been mined all over the world for centuries. It is also sometimes mined for its silver content. Austria, Germany, England, Mexico, and Peru are some of the important sites for tetrahedrite.

| | |
|---|---|
| **HARDNESS** | 3–4 |
| **SG** | 4.6–5.1 |
| **COLOUR** | Flint-grey to iron-black |
| **TRANSPARENCY** | Opaque |
| **LUSTRE** | Metallic |

## yrargyrite

rargyrite is
important
urce of silver.
so called dark
oy silver, it
rkens when
posed to
nt. Its name
rives from the
eek words *pyr*, meaning
e", and *argent*, meaning "silver".

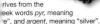

| HARDNESS 2.5 | SG 5.8 |
|---|---|
| OLOUR Deep red | |
| RANSPARENCY Translucent | |
| USTRE Diamondlike | |

## Proustite

Proustite is sensitive to light and turns
from transparent scarlet to opaque grey
when exposed to strong light. Its bright
wine-red crystals make attractive gems. Chile
and Germany are notable sources of this mineral.

| HARDNESS 2–2.5 |
|---|
| SG 5.8 |
| COLOUR Scarlet, grey |
| TRANSPARENCY Translucent |
| LUSTRE Diamondlike to submetallic |

## ournonite

A combination of copper, lead,
antimony, and sulphur, bournonite forms
tablet-shaped prismatic crystals. Some of
the crystals found in the mineral-rich Harz
Mountains of Germany have a diameter
of 2.5 cm (1 in) or more. It has been
nicknamed "cogwheel ore" as it
sometimes develops crystals in
the shape of a cogwheel.

| HARDNESS 2.5–3 |
|---|
| SG 5.8 |
| COLOUR Steel-grey |
| TRANSPARENCY Opaque |
| LUSTRE Metallic |

# Oxides

These minerals form when oxygen combines with a metal or semi-metal. In simple oxides, only a single metal or semi-metal is present, but multiple oxides may contain several.

FOCUS ON...
## MAJOR ORE
Some minerals are mined as ores as the contain useful eleme such as metals.

## Ruby

Known in Sanskrit as *ratnaraj* or "king of precious stones", ruby is the red variety of corundum, the hardest mineral on Earth after diamond. Heating improves its colour and clarity. Crystals of ruby tend to be small, as the presence of chromium hampers their growth. Therefore, large rubies have high value. Several myths and beliefs are associated with ruby. In Burmese tradition, ruby bestows good fortune and invincibility, and Russians traditionally consider it to be good for the heart, brain, blood purification, and vitality.

| HARDNESS | 9 | SG | 4–4.1 |
|---|---|---|---|

**COLOUR**  Red

**TRANSPARENCY**
Transparent to translucent

**LUSTRE**  Diamondlike to glassy

The mineral cuprite is an ore
copper – which is widely used
making electrical wires.

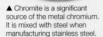

▲ Chromite is a significant
source of the metal chromium.
It is mixed with steel when
manufacturing stainless steel.

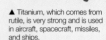

▲ Titanium, which comes from
rutile, is very strong and is used
in aircraft, spacecraft, missiles,
and ships.

## Sapphire

Another variety of corundum is sapphire. It is most
abundant in metamorphic rocks, and large deposits
are quite rare. This oxide is "pleochroic", which
means it appears in different colours when viewed
from different angles. Despite their hardness,
sapphires are also carved or engraved. The
423-carat Logan Sapphire, mined in Sri Lanka, is
believed to be the world's largest blue sapphire.

| | | | |
|---|---|---|---|
| **HARDNESS** 9 | | **SG** 4–4.1 | |
| **COLOUR** Occurs in most colours | | | |
| **TRANSPARENCY** Transparent to translucent | | | |
| **LUSTRE** Diamondlike to glassy | | | |

Colour may
be patchy

Glassy lustre

## Magnetite

This mineral is so highly magnetic, it will attract iron and can move a compass needle. The ancient Chinese made their first compasses with magnetite.

| HARDNESS 5.5–6 | SG 5.2 |
|---|---|
| COLOUR Black to brownish-black | |
| TRANSPARENCY Opaque | |
| LUSTRE Metallic to semi-metallic | |

## Spinel

The red variety of this mineral is hard and is cut as a gemstone. It looks similar to ruby – the Black Prince's Ruby in the British Imperial State Crown was found to be a spinel.

| HARDNESS 7.5–8 | SG 3.6 |
|---|---|
| COLOUR Red, yellow, orange-red, blue, green, brown, black | |
| TRANSPARENCY Transparent to translucent | |
| LUSTRE Glassy | |

## Cassiterite

A tin oxide, cassiterite derives its name from *kassiteros*, the Greek word for "tin". It is a major source of tin and is found in China, Malaysia, and Indonesia.

| HARDNESS 6–7 | SG 7 |
|---|---|
| COLOUR Medium to dark brown | |
| TRANSPARENCY Transparent to opaque | |
| LUSTRE Diamondlike to metallic | |

## Zincite

Also known as red oxide of zinc, zincite rarely forms crystals. It is found in Sterling Hill, New Jersey, USA.

*Zincite*

| HARDNESS 4 | |
|---|---|
| SG 5.7 | |
| COLOUR Orange-yellow to deep red | |
| TRANSPARENCY Almost opaque | |
| LUSTRE Resinous | |

# hromite

Chromite is the major source of chromium. This metal is mixed with iron to make high-speed tools and stainless steel.

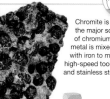

**ARDNESS** 5.5 **SG** 4.7
**OLOUR** Dark brown, black
**ANSPARENCY** Opaque
**STRE** Metallic

# Chrysoberyl

This mineral has been used in Asia for thousands of years as an amulet to protect against "the evil eye". Its gemstone variety, alexandrite, is one of the rarest and most expensive gems.

**HARDNESS** 8.5
**SG** 3.7
**COLOUR** Green, yellow
**TRANSPARENCY** Transparent to translucent
**LUSTRE** Glassy

# ematite

matite is the most important ore of n. Its name is derived from the Greek *matitis*, meaning "blood-red" – a reference the red colour of its powder. It has long been sociated with blood – bones of Neolithic burials ve been found smeared with hematite powder.

**ARDNESS** 5–6 **SG** 5.3
**OLOUR** Steel-grey
**ANSPARENCY** aque
**STRE** etallic dull

# Perovskite

Found in Earth's upper mantle, Perovskite was first discovered in the Ural Mountains of Russia.

**HARDNESS** 5.5
**SG** 4
**COLOUR** Black, brown, yellow
**TRANSPARENCY** Transparent to opaque
**LUSTRE** Diamondlike, metallic

## Uraninite

A radioactive mineral, uraninite is the main source of uranium, which is used to power nuclear reactors. In earlier times, it was used in small amounts for colouring ceramics.

| | | |
|---|---|---|
| **HARDNESS** 5–6 | **SG** 6.5–11 | |

**COLOUR** Black to brownish-black, dark grey, greenish

**TRANSPARENCY** Opaque

**LUSTRE** Submetallic, pitchy, dull

## Samarskite

Named after Russian mining engineer Vasili Samarski-Bykhovets, samarskite contains uranium and has radioactive crystals. It was discovered in Miass, Russia.

| | |
|---|---|
| **HARDNESS** 5–6 | **SG** 5.7 |

**COLOUR** Black

**TRANSPARENCY** Translucent to opaque

**LUSTRE** Glassy to resinous

## Brookite

This mineral is named after English crystallographer H J Brooke. It is one of the few naturally occurring polymorphs (a mineral that can crystallize in different forms).

| | |
|---|---|
| **HARDNESS** 5.5–6 | **SG** 4.1 |

**COLOUR** Various shades of brown

**TRANSPARENCY** Opaque to transparent

**LUSTRE** Metallic to diamondlike

Brooki

# yrochlore

is mineral gets its name from Greek
ords for "fire" and "green" because it turns
een after heating. It is an important source of
obium, a soft grey metal used mostly in alloys
ch as steel.

| HARDNESS | 5–5.5 |
| SG | 4.5 |
| COLOUR | Brown to black |
| TRANSPARENCY | Translucent to opaque |
| LUSTRE | Glassy to resinous |

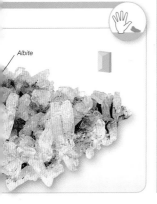

Albite

# Rutile

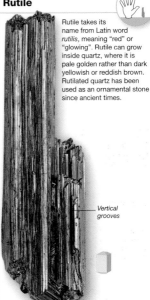

Rutile takes its
name from Latin word
*rutilis*, meaning "red" or
"glowing". Rutile can grow
inside quartz, where it is
pale golden rather than dark
yellowish or reddish brown.
Rutilated quartz has been
used as an ornamental stone
since ancient times.

Vertical
grooves

| HARDNESS | 6–6.5 | SG | 4.2 |
| COLOUR | Reddish-brown to red | | |
| TRANSPARENCY | Transparent to opaque | | |
| LUSTRE | Diamondlike to submetallic | | |

# Hydroxides

Hydroxides form when a metal combines with water and oxygen at a low temperature. They are usually found in sedimentary rock and are often important ore minerals. Many hydroxide minerals are very soft.

### Diaspore

Diaspore takes its name from the Greek word for "scatter", because when it is heated, it crackles and scatters light. This makes it look as though it has different colours when seen from different angles.

| | | |
|---|---|---|
| **HARDNESS** 6.5–7 | **SG** 3.4 | |
| **COLOUR** White, grey, yellow, lilac, or pink | | |
| **TRANSPARENCY** Transparent to translucent | | |
| **LUSTRE** Glassy | | |

### Bauxite

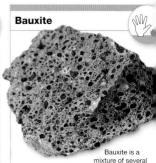

Bauxite is a mixture of several minerals that include aluminium oxides or hydroxides. Technically it is a rock, but it's usually grouped with minerals. It is an importa[nt] source of aluminium. Of all the bauxite mined, 90 per cent is used to extract aluminium.

| | | |
|---|---|---|
| **HARDNESS** 1–3 | **SG** 2.3–2.7 | |
| **COLOUR** White, yellowish, red, reddish-brow[n] | | |
| **TRANSPARENCY** Opaque | | |
| **LUSTRE** Earthy | | |

# oethite

German poet and author Johann Wolfgang von Goethe was an enthusiastic mineralogist, and goethite is named after him. It is an iron oxide hydroxide and can occur as grooved crystals.

| | |
|---|---|
| **HARDNESS** | 5–5.5 |
| **SG** | 4.3 |
| **COLOUR** | Orangish to blackish-brown |
| **TRANSPARENCY** | Translucent to opaque |
| **LUSTRE** | Diamondlike to metallic |

# imonite

monite has been used as a pigment painting since ancient Egyptian nes, and was also used by the Dutch ortrait artist Anthony van Dyck. It rms as a secondary mineral when her minerals oxidize (react with xygen), and doesn't form crystals.

| | |
|---|---|
| **ARDNESS** | 4–5.5 |
| **G** | 2.7–4.3 |
| **OLOUR** | Various shades brown, yellow |
| **RANSPARENCY** | Opaque |
| **USTRE** | Earthy, sometimes bmetallic or dull |

# Halides

Halides are soft minerals and have a low specific gravity. These minerals form when metals combine with one of the common halogen elements, which include fluorine, chlorine, bromine, and iodine.

### Halite

Halite is common edible salt, or sodium chloride. A vital mineral for human and animal health, salt is also used as a preservative and in making soap and glass. Halite forms as salty deposits when saltwater evaporates, and is found worldwide.

| HARDNESS 2.5 | SG 2.1–2.6 |
|---|---|
| COLOUR Colourless to white | |
| TRANSPARENCY Transparent to translucent | |
| LUSTRE Glassy | |

# Fluorite

luorite melts easily, and its name
omes from the Latin *fluere*, "to flow".
hen seen under ultraviolet light, this mineral
fluorescent (it gives off a glowing light).

**ARDNESS** 4    **SG** 3.2–3.6

**OLOUR** Occurs in
ost colours

**RANSPARENCY**
ansparent to
anslucent

**USTRE**
lassy

# Cryolite

Molten cryolite was mixed with
aluminium oxides for the manufacture
of aircraft and engineering products.

**HARDNESS** 2.5    **SG** 3

**COLOUR** Colourless to snow-white

**TRANSPARENCY**
Transparent to
translucent

**LUSTRE**
Glassy to
greasy

# Carnallite

arnallite forms when potassium and
agnesium chloride mix with water. It is
n important source of the chemical potash.

**HARDNESS** 2.5    **SG** 1.6

**COLOUR** Milky white, often reddish

**RANSPARENCY** Translucent to opaque

**USTRE** Greasy

# Atacamite

The Statue
of Liberty in
New York, USA, is
coloured green
by a layer of
atacamite. It is
named after the
Atacama Desert
in Chile.

**HARDNESS** 3–3.5    **SG** 3.8

**COLOUR** Bright green to blackish-green

**TRANSPARENCY** Transparent to translucent

**LUSTRE** Diamondlike to glassy

The world's largest salt flat,
Salar de Uyuni contains around

# 10 billion

tonnes of salt

**HALITE**
Large crystals of halite, or common salt, forms after the evaporation of water from the sea or saltwater lakes. Salar de Uyuni, in Bolivia, is the remains of a prehistoric salt lake. It covers an area of 10,582 sq km (4,086 sq miles).

# Carbonates

Carbonate minerals form when a carbonate (carbon and oxygen) combines with metals or semi-metals. They can be found in sea shells, coral reefs, and rocks such as marble and chalk.

### FOCUS ON...
## CALCITE
Most carbonates fou[n] in Earth's crust are calcite – a useful for[m] of calcium carbonat[e]

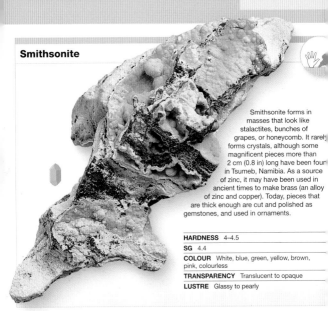

### Smithsonite

Smithsonite forms in masses that look like stalactites, bunches of grapes, or honeycomb. It rarel[y] forms crystals, although some magnificent pieces more than 2 cm (0.8 in) long have been foun[d] in Tsumeb, Namibia. As a source of zinc, it may have been used in ancient times to make brass (an alloy of zinc and copper). Today, pieces that are thick enough are cut and polished as gemstones, and used in ornaments.

| HARDNESS | 4–4.5 |
|---|---|
| SG | 4.4 |
| COLOUR | White, blue, green, yellow, brown, pink, colourless |
| TRANSPARENCY | Translucent to opaque |
| LUSTRE | Glassy to pearly |

White and yellow cite was quarried in ient Egypt and used uildings and statues.

▲ Marble is another form of calcite. Strong and decorative, it is still used in buildings today.

▲ Found inside caves, calcite forms long, thin stalactites that build up as water drips.

▲ Calcium carbonate taken from calcite is the main ingredient for indigestion tablets.

## Calcite

ne of the three most common arbonates on Earth, this calcium arbonate grows anywhere that water can reach. nellfish make their shells from calcite, which ey take from sea water. Calcite is known for its eautiful crystals, and although it can be almost y colour, in its pure form it is white or colourless.

**ARDNESS** 3

**G** 2.7

**OLOUR** Colourless, hite, yellow, black, green

**RANSPARENCY**
ransparent to anslucent

**USTRE**
assy

## Siderite

This shiny mineral is an iron carbonate and takes its name from the Greek *sideros*, meaning "iron". Its crystals often have curved faces. When heated, siderite becomes magnetic.

| **HARDNESS** 3.5–4 | **SG** 3.9 |
| --- | --- |
| **COLOUR** Yellowish-brown to dark brown | |
| **TRANSPARENCY** Translucent | |
| **LUSTRE** Glassy to pearly | |

## Aragonite

Formed at low temperatures near Earth's surface, aragonite is found in caves and around hot springs. It forms different shapes, including one that resembles coral. In this shape it is called *flos-ferri*, meaning "flowers of iron".

| | |
|---|---|
| **HARDNESS** | 3.5–4 |
| **SG** | 2.9 |
| **COLOUR** | Colourless, white, grey, yellowish, reddish, green |
| **TRANSPARENCY** | Transparent to translucent |
| **LUSTRE** | Glassy inclining to resinous |

## Malachite

Malachite is possibly one of the oldest known sources of copper. In ancient Egypt, it was used as an eye paint, probably to prevent eye infections.

| | | | |
|---|---|---|---|
| **HARDNESS** | 3.5–4 | **SG** | 3.9–4 |
| **COLOUR** | Bright green | | |
| **TRANSPARENCY** | Translucent | | |
| **LUSTRE** | Diamondlike to silky | | |

## Rhodochrosite

Gem-quality crystals of this manganese carbonate can be found in the USA and South Africa. These are sometimes cut for collectors. The more common form has a band of colours and is used as decorative stone.

The Incas believed rhodochrosite was the blood of ancient kings and queens that had turned to stone.

| HARDNESS | 3.5–4 | SG | 3.8 |
| --- | --- | --- | --- |

**COLOUR** Rose-pink, brown or grey

**TRANSPARENCY** Transparent to translucent

**LUSTRE** Glassy to pearly

## Aurichalcite

Aurichalcite is Latin for "golden copper". It has a distinctive velvetlike coating. It burns with a green flame because it contains copper.

| HARDNESS | 1–2 | SG | 4.2 |
| --- | --- | --- | --- |

**COLOUR** Sky-blue, green-blue, or pale green

**TRANSPARENCY** Transparent to translucent

**LUSTRE** Silky to pearly

## Ankerite

Harder than a piece of copper, but softer than steel, ankerite forms distinctive curved crystals. It is a rare mineral and is not mined for any specific purpose.

| HARDNESS | 3.5–4 | SG | 2.9 |
| --- | --- | --- | --- |

**COLOUR** Colourless to pale buff

**TRANSPARENCY** Translucent

**LUSTRE** Glassy to pearly

## Barytocalcite

This mineral is made up of barium and calcite. Its surface is covered in grooves and ridges that look like dog's teeth. It is often found within limestone and produces bubbles when put in hydrochloric acid.

**HARDNESS** 4     **SG** 3.7

**COLOUR** White, greyish, greenish, or yellowish

**TRANSPARENCY** Transparent to translucent

**LUSTRE** Glassy to resinous

## Dolomite

This common mineral is recognized by its curved saddle-shaped crystals. It is an important rock-forming mineral and also a minor source of magnesium.

**HARDNESS** 3.5-4

**SG** 2.8-2.9

**COLOUR** Colourless, white, or cream

**TRANSPARENCY** Transparent to translucent

**LUSTRE** Glassy

## Magnesite

It is almost impossible to melt magnesite, making it ideal for lining furnaces. It is also used in the production of synthetic rubber.

**HARDNESS** 4

**SG** 3

**COLOUR** White, light grey, yellowish, brownish

**TRANSPARENCY** Transparent to translucent

**LUSTRE** Glassy

## Phosgenite

This rare carbonate forms close to Earth's surface when lead-rich minerals react with water. It is named after the colourless and poisonous gas phosgene, as they are both made up of carbon, oxygen, and chlorine.

**HARDNESS** 2.5–3     **SG** 6.1

**COLOUR** White, yellow, brown, or gre[...]

**TRANSPARENCY** Transparent to translucent

**LUSTRE** Resinous

## zurite

urite takes its name from the Persian *hudward*, meaning "blue". In the 15th 17th centuries, it was used as a natural ouring pigment in European art. It is also one the sources of copper.

**RDNESS** 3.5–4

**a** 3.8

**OLOUR**
ure to dark blue

**ANSPARENCY**
nsparent to nslucent

**STRE**
assy to dull earthy

## Artinite

Artinite forms fluffy balls of needle-shaped crystals. It dissolves in cold acids, giving off water and carbon dioxide.

| | |
|---|---|
| **HARDNESS** 2.5 | **SG** 2 |
| **COLOUR** White | |
| **TRANSPARENCY** Transparent | |
| **LUSTRE** Glassy | |

*Small radiating crystal*

## trontianite

e crystals of this mineral are short, umnar, and needle-shaped. It is the in source of strontium and is used in sugar ning for extracting sugar from sugarcane.

**RDNESS** 3.5–4     **SG** 3.7

**LOUR** Colourless, grey, green, ow, or reddish

**ANSPARENCY**
nsparent to slucent

**STRE**
ssy

## Trona

Trona takes it name from the Arabic *natrun*, meaning "salt". It is usually found on the surface of Earth in powdery form, especially in dry, salty desert areas. It is also a source of sodium.

| | |
|---|---|
| **HARDNESS** 2.5–3 | **SG** 2.1 |
| **COLOUR** Colourless to grey, yellow-white | |
| **TRANSPARENCY** Transparent to translucent | |
| **LUSTRE** Glassy, glistening | |

# Phosphates, arsenates, and vanadates

These minerals are grouped together because they have similar patterns of atoms. The most abundant of the three are phosphates, with more than 200 known types.

## Variscite

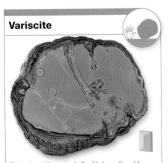

This mineral is named after Varisca, the old name for the German district of Voightland where variscite was first found. It is sometimes worn as jewellery, but it is porous and can absorb the body's natural oils, which discolour it.

| HARDNESS | 4.5 | SG | 2.6 |
|---|---|---|---|
| COLOUR | Pale to apple-green | | |
| TRANSPARENCY | Opaque | | |
| LUSTRE | Glassy to waxy | | |

## Pyromorphite

A minor ore of lead, this phosphate occurs in the oxidized zone of lead deposits. Pyromorph gets its name from the Greek word *pyr*, meanin "fire", and *morphe*, meaning "form". It is so named because it forms crystals on cooling after being melted.

| HARDNESS | 3.5–4 | SG | 7 |
|---|---|---|---|
| COLOUR | Green, yellow, orange, or brown | | |
| TRANSPARENCY | Transparent to translucent | | |
| LUSTRE | Resinous | | |

## avellite

Radiating crystal

vellite contains a mixture of oxygen, minium, and phosphorus. It forms balls rystals in chert rock, limestone, and granite. en these balls are broken, they reveal clike patterns.

| RDNESS | 3.5–4 | SG | 2.4 |
|---|---|---|---|
| LOUR | Green or white | | |
| ANSPARENCY | Translucent | | |
| STRE | Glassy to resinous | | |

## Turquoise

One of the first gemstones to be mined, turquoise varies from sky-blue to green depending on the amount of iron or copper in it. Turquoise was the national gemstone of Persia (now Iran). The Persians believed that seeing the reflection of a new moon on a turquoise stone brought good luck.

| HARDNESS | 5–6 | SG | 2.6–2.8 |
|---|---|---|---|
| COLOUR | Blue, green | | |
| TRANSPARENCY | Usually opaque | | |
| LUSTRE | Waxy to dull | | |

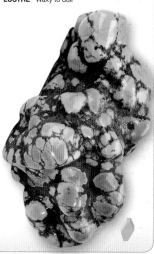

## Apatite

Apatite is a name given to a group of minerals that contain calcium and phosphorus. It is used to make many thin including matches. Apatite derives its na from the Greek word *apate,* which mea "deceit", because it looks similar to other minerals, including amethyst, aquamarine, and olivine.

| | |
|---|---|
| **HARDNESS** | 5 |
| **SG** | 3.1–3.2 |
| **COLOUR** | Green, blue, violet, purp colourless, yellow, or rose |
| **TRANSPARENCY** | Transparent to translucent |
| **LUSTRE** | Glassy, waxy |

## Carnotite

A radioactive mineral, carnotite is an important source of uranium, and gives off radium gas.

| | | | |
|---|---|---|---|
| **HARDNESS** | 2 | **SG** | 4.7 |
| **COLOUR** | Yellow | | |
| **TRANSPARENCY** | Semi-transparent to opaque | | |
| **LUSTRE** | Pearly to dull | | |

## Chalcophyllite

This mineral is named after the Greek words for "copper" and "leaf" because it contains copper and grows in a leaflike pattern. Easy to mould, copper has been cast since 4,000 BCE.

| | | | |
|---|---|---|---|
| **HARDNESS** | 2 | **SG** | 2.7 |
| **COLOUR** | Vivid blue-green | | |
| **TRANSPARENCY** | Transparent to transluce | | |
| **LUSTRE** | Pearly to glassy | | |

## damite

s mineral is generally highly
prescent – when viewed under
aviolet light, it gives off amazing colours. It
s no commercial use but its bright and lustrous
stals are sought by mineral collectors.

| RDNESS 3.5 | SG 4.4 |
|---|---|
| | COLOUR Yellow, green, pink or violet |
| | TRANSPARENCY Transparent to translucent |
| | LUSTRE Glassy |

## Erythrite

This brightly
coloured mineral
is commonly called
cobalt bloom. It is an
ore of cobalt, nickel, and
silver. Some of the best
erythrite is found in
Canada and Morocco.

| HARDNESS 1.5–2.5 |
|---|
| SG 3.1 |
| COLOUR Purple-pink |
| TRANSPARENCY Transparent to translucent |
| LUSTRE Diamondlike to glassy, pearly |

## imetite

netite deposits are found where lead and
enic occur together. Its name is derived
m the Greek *mimetes*, meaning "imitator",
cause of its resemblance to pyromorphite.

| RDNESS 3.5–4 |
|---|
| 7.3 |
| LOUR Pale yellow to owish-brown, orange, green |
| ANSPARENCY Subtransparent |
| STRE Resinous |

This Aztec funeral mask is made of turquoise, gold, and shell overlaid on a

# human skull

# Nitrates and borates

These minerals are formed when oxygen combines with nitrogen and boron respectively. They have low specific gravity and are usually soft.

## Borax

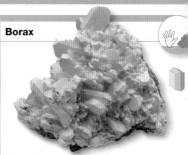

The name borax comes from the Arabic *buraq*, which means "white". It is an evaporite mineral that forms in large desert lake beds, and contains sodium and boron. Borax can fuse or melt easily to become colourless glass, and is also a source of boron.

| | | | |
|---|---|---|---|
| **HARDNESS** 2–2.5 | | **SG** 1.7 | |
| **COLOUR** Colourless | | | |
| **TRANSPARENCY** Transparent to translucent | | | |
| **LUSTRE** Glassy to earthy | | | |

# Howlite

Howlite is named after its discoverer,
Canadian chemist Henry How. It
can be dyed and used in place of
turquoise, although it is not as hard
as turquoise and lacks depth of colour.
Significant deposits of howlite are
found in Death Valley, California, USA.

| | | | |
|---|---|---|---|
| **HARDNESS** 3.5 | | **SG** 2.6 |
| **COLOUR** White | | |
| **TRANSPARENCY** Translucent opaque | | |
| **LUSTRE** Almost glassy | | |

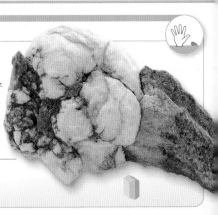

# Nitratine

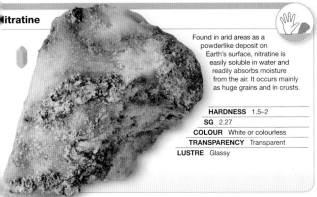

Found in arid areas as a
powderlike deposit on
Earth's surface, nitratine is
easily soluble in water and
readily absorbs moisture
from the air. It occurs mainly
as huge grains and in crusts.

| | |
|---|---|
| **HARDNESS** 1.5–2 | |
| **SG** 2.27 | |
| **COLOUR** White or colourless | |
| **TRANSPARENCY** Transparent | |
| **LUSTRE** Glassy | |

# Sulphates, chromates, molybdates, tungstates

Oxygen combines with sulphur, chromium, molybdenum, and tungsten respectively to form these minerals. In their concentrated form they are valuable ores of the metal or semi-metal they contai

## Crocoite

Crocoite takes its name from the Greek word for "saffron", which is a reference to its brilliant colour. However, it loses its sheen when exposed to light. Fine crocoite specimens are found in Tasmania, Australia, and it is the official mineral emblem of the island.

| | |
|---|---|
| **HARDNESS** | 2.5–3 |
| **SG** | 6 |
| **COLOUR** | Orange, red |
| **TRANSPARENCY** | Transparent to translucent |
| **LUSTRE** | Glassy |

**OCUS ON...**
**YPSUM**
s common
phate is widely
ed, especially in
ilding and design.

▲ Gypsum is used for making plaster of Paris and mortar and also as an adhesive in industrial processes.

▲ Alabaster, a fine-grained form of gypsum, is used for carvings and ornamental purposes.

**Wulfenite**

amed after mineralogist F X Wulfen, this neral is often found with lead ores and is minor source of molybdenum. Its unique uare-shaped crystals look like interlocking astic tiles. Large crystals come from Mexico, SA, Zambia, China, and Slovenia.

| HARDNESS | 2.5–3 | SG | 6.5–7 |
|---|---|---|---|
| **COLOUR** | Yellow, orange, red | | |
| **TRANSPARENCY** | Transparent to translucent | | |
| **LUSTRE** | Diamondlike to greasy | | |

## Ferberite

Ferberite is named after German mineralogist Dr Moritz Rudolph Ferber. It is an iron tungstate that usually occurs as flat, stepped crystals, and is an ore of tungsten. This very useful metal is used in electric-light filaments.

| HARDNESS 4–4.5 | SG 7.5 |
| --- | --- |
| COLOUR Black | |
| TRANSPARENCY Opaque | |
| LUSTRE Submetallic | |

## Chalcanthite

## Gypsum

Gypsum is formed when seawater evaporates. Such surface-forming minerals are usually soft. An extremely common substance, gypsum is mined on a large scale in many parts of the world. Plaster of Paris, alabaster, fertilizers, and some types of explosives contain gypsum.

| HARDNESS 2 | SG 2.3 |
| --- | --- |
| COLOUR Colourless, white, light brown, yellow, pink | |
| TRANSPARENCY Transparent to translucent | |
| LUSTRE Almost glassy to pearly | |

...halcanthite dissolves easily in water and is, therefore, more common in dry regions. It used to be known as blue vitriol, but is now named for the Greek words for "copper" and "flower". It is an important ore of copper especially in dry regions such as Chile.

| | |
|---|---|
| **HARDNESS** 2.5 | |
| **SG** 2.3 | |
| **COLOUR** Blue | |
| **TRANSPARENCY** Transparent | |
| **LUSTRE** Glassy | |

## Brochantite

This mineral is named after French geologist A J M Brochant de Villiers. It is a source of copper. The needle-like crystals of brochantite are a few millimetres long, but magnificent specimens 10 mm long are found in Namibia and Arizona, USA.

| | |
|---|---|
| **HARDNESS** 3.5–4 | **SG** 4 |
| **COLOUR** Emerald-green | |
| **TRANSPARENCY** Translucent | |
| **LUSTRE** Glassy | |

## Scheelite

...paque crystals of scheelite weighing ...p to 7 kg (15 lb) are found in Arizona. It is a major source of tungsten. The nozzle of the Saturn V rocket, which launched *Apollo 11* in 1969, was made of tungsten-steel.

| | |
|---|---|
| **HARDNESS** 4.5–5 | **SG** 6.1 |
| **COLOUR** White, yellow, brown, green | |
| **TRANSPARENCY** Transparent to translucent | |
| **LUSTRE** Glassy to greasy | |

## Baryte

Also known as heavy spar, this mineral gets its name from *barys*, the Greek word for "heavy", because it has a high specific gravity. It is the main source of barium, and is used in oil and gas wells, in paper, and in cloth-making.

| | |
|---|---|
| **HARDNESS** 3–3.5 | |
| **SG** 4.5 | |
| **COLOUR** Colourless, white, grey, bluish, greenish, beige | |
| **TRANSPARENCY** Transparent to translucent | |
| **LUSTRE** Glassy, resinous, pearly | |

# Silicates

The biggest group of minerals, silicates are found in abundance and are the main components of igneous and metamorphic rocks. Made of silicon and oxygen, they are usually hard, transparent, and are moderately dense.

## FOCUS ON...
### GEMSTONES

Several silicates are used as gemstones because of their colourful crystals.

▶ Jade is a tough mineral, which makes it ideal for carving.

▲ Precious opal can form only in undisturbed space within another rock.

▲ The ancient Egyptians believed that topaz was coloured in the glow of the Sun god Ra.

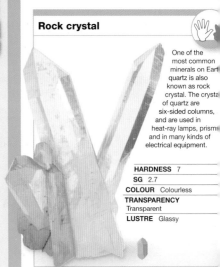

### Rock crystal

One of the most common minerals on Earth, quartz is also known as rock crystal. The crystals of quartz are six-sided columns, and are used in heat-ray lamps, prisms, and in many kinds of electrical equipment.

| HARDNESS | 7 |
|---|---|
| SG | 2.7 |
| COLOUR | Colourless |
| TRANSPARENCY | Transparent |
| LUSTRE | Glassy |

# Amethyst

Purple quartz is called amethyst, named after the maiden Amethyst from Greek mythology. Amethyst was very popular in 19th-century jewellery. Its colour comes from tiny quantities of iron in it. Some amethyst crystals turn yellow-brown when heated. These are often sold as citrine.

| | |
|---|---|
| **HARDNESS** | 7 |
| **SG** | 2.7 |
| **COLOUR** | Violet |
| **TRANSPARENCY** | Opaque to translucent |
| **LUSTRE** | Glassy |

# Citrine

The name citrine comes from the Latin word *citrina*, meaning "yellow". It gets its colour from the iron oxide present in it. The mineral is also known as gold topaz.

| | |
|---|---|
| **HARDNESS** | 7 |
| **SG** | 2.7 |
| **COLOUR** | Yellow, yellow-brown |
| **TRANSPARENCY** | Translucent to nearly opaque |
| **LUSTRE** | Glassy |

# Rose quartz

The pink variety of quartz is known as rose quartz. It has been carved since ancient times. Today, "crystal healers" believe that this mineral can bring unconditional love if worn against the skin.

| | | |
|---|---|---|
| **HARDNESS** | 7 | **SG** 2.65 |
| **COLOUR** | Various, including pink and rose | |
| **TRANSPARENCY** | Translucent to nearly opaque | |
| **LUSTRE** | Glassy | |

## Agate

Agate is the banded variety of chalcedony, a fine-grained quartz. It usually grows in rings around a common centre, in rock cavities or extrusive igneous rocks.

| HARDNESS | 6.5–7 | SG | 2.6 |
|---|---|---|---|

| COLOUR | Colourless, white, yellow, grey, brown, blue, or red |
|---|---|

| TRANSPARENCY | Translucent to opaque |
|---|---|

| LUSTRE | Glassy to waxy |
|---|---|

## Onyx

Onyx is the striped, semiprecious variety of agate with alternating bands of colour. The layers of contrasting colours make it an ideal material for carving jewellery.

*Translucent brown sard*

| HARDNESS | 6.5–7 |
|---|---|

| SG | 2.6 |
|---|---|

| COLOUR | Different colours |
|---|---|

| TRANSPARENCY | Translucent to nearly opaque |
|---|---|

| LUSTRE | Glassy |
|---|---|

## Bloodstone

According to ancient Greek lore, bloodstone was a preserver of health and offered protection against nosebleeds, anger, and discord. Bloodstones are named for their red spots, which resemble drops of blood.

| HARDNESS | 6.5–7 | SG | 2.6 |
|---|---|---|---|

| | COLOUR | Different colours with red spots |
|---|---|---|

| | TRANSPARENCY | Translucent to opaque |
|---|---|---|

| | LUSTRE | Glassy |
|---|---|---|

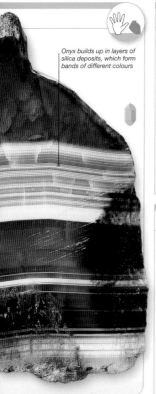

Onyx builds up in layers of silica deposits, which form bands of different colours

## Opal

Opal occurs in many forms and many different crystal shapes. It is used as a semiprecious gemstone, and is chiefly found in Australia.

| HARDNESS 5–6 | SG 1.9–2.3 |
|---|---|

**COLOUR** Colourless, white, yellow, orange, rose-red, black, or dark blue

**TRANSPARENCY** Transparent to translucent

**LUSTRE** Glassy

## Sard

A translucent mineral, sard has been used since ancient times for making cameos and jewellery. It was used at Harappa, one of the oldest centres of the Indus civilization (c. 2,300–1,500 BCE).

| HARDNESS 6.5–7 | SG 2.6 |
|---|---|

**COLOUR** Light to dark-brown

**TRANSPARENCY** Translucent to opaque

**LUSTRE** Glassy

## Lazurite

This rare mineral forms in limestone and it is the main mineral in lapis lazuli – a rock prized for its use in carvings, medicines, cosmetics, and jewellery for thousands of years. Lazurite is also the main ingredient of a brilliant blue pigment called ultramarine. The best lazurite crystals come from Afghanistan.

| | |
|---|---|
| **HARDNESS**  5–5.5 | **SG**  2.4 |

| | |
|---|---|
| **COLOUR**  Various intense shades of blue | |

| | |
|---|---|
| **TRANSPARENCY**  Translucent to opaque | |

| | |
|---|---|
| **LUSTRE**  Dull to glassy | |

## Leucite

The Greek word *leukos*, meaning "white", gives leucite its name – a reference to its most common colour. Leucite occurs only in igneous rocks, mainly those that are potassium-rich and silica-poor.

| | |
|---|---|
| **HARDNESS**  5.5–6 | **SG**  2.5 |

| | |
|---|---|
| **COLOUR**  White, grey, or colourless | |

| | |
|---|---|
| **TRANSPARENCY** Transparent to translucent | |

| | |
|---|---|
| **LUSTRE**  Glassy | |

Leucite

Bedrock

# Orthoclase

A major rock-forming mineral, orthoclase's pink crystals give granite its characteristic colour. This mineral is important in ceramics, where it is used as a clay for making objects and as a glaze. Moonstone, the smooth and shiny variety of orthoclase, was regarded as sacred in India.

| | | | |
|---|---|---|---|
| **HARDNESS** 6 | | **SG** 2.5–2.6 | |

**COLOUR** Colourless, white, cream, yellow, pink, brown-red

**TRANSPARENCY** Transparent to translucent

**LUSTRE** Glassy

# Cancrinite

This silicate was found originally in the Ural Mountains in Russia. It forms in a number of igneous rocks. Cancrinite rarely forms crystals, although they may grow to several centimetres wide.

| | | |
|---|---|---|
| **HARDNESS** 5–6 | | **SG** 2.5 |

**COLOUR** Pale to dark yellow, orange, violet, pink, or purple

**TRANSPARENCY** Transparent to translucent

**LUSTRE** Glassy

## Topaz

This mineral's name was probably inspired by the Sanskrit word *tapas*, which means "fire" – a reference to its golden-yellow colour. Topaz also exists in other colours. It is classified as a gemstone because of its beautiful and rare crystals.

| HARDNESS | 8 | SG | 3.4–3.6 |
|---|---|---|---|

**COLOUR** Colourless, blue, yellow, pink, brown, green

**TRANSPARENCY** Transparent to translucent

**LUSTRE** Glassy

## Grossular

## Zircon

This mineral often matches diamond in its sparkling brilliance. Some crystals of zircon found in Mount Narryer in western Australia are almost 4.4 billion years old.

| HARDNESS | 7.5 | SG | 4.6–4.7 |
|---|---|---|---|

**COLOUR** Colourless, brown, red, yellow, orange, blue, green

**TRANSPARENCY** Transparent to opaque

**LUSTRE** Diamondlike to oily

## Kyanite

This silicate has been used to make heat-resistant porcelains, such as used in spark plugs. Gem-quality kyanite crystals are found in Bahia, Brazil. Its name is an adaptation of the Greek word *kyanos*, meaning "dark blue" – a reference to one of its many colour forms.

| HARDNESS | 4.5–6 |
|---|---|
| SG | 3.6 |
| COLOUR | Blue, green |

**TRANSPARENCY** Transparent to translucent

**LUSTRE** Glassy

This type of garnet is commonly found in calcium-rich metamorphic rocks, and has been found in meteorites. Green grossular, also known as tsavolite, comes from Tanzania.

**HARDNESS** 6.5–7

**SG** 3.6

**COLOUR** Wide range of colours

**TRANSPARENCY** Transparent to translucent

**LUSTRE** Glassy

# Andalusite

Andalusite is usually found in metamorphic rocks. Sometimes its crystals grow together trapping dark, carbon-based matter in between, which forms a cross when seen in cross-section.

**HARDNESS** 6.5–7.5 **SG** 3.2

**COLOUR** Pink, brown, white, grey, violet, yellow, green, blue

**TRANSPARENCY** Transparent to nearly opaque

**LUSTRE** Glassy

# Sillimanite

This is named after Professor Benjamin Silliman, a geologist, chemist, and founder of the *American Journal of Science*. Sillimanite is commonly used to make heat-resistant porcelain.

**HARDNESS** 7

**SG** 3.2–3.3

**COLOUR** Colourless, white, pale yellow, blue, green, violet

**TRANSPARENCY** Transparent to translucent

**LUSTRE** Silky

## Olivine

Olivine refers to a group of silicate minerals that
form in molten rock beneath Earth's surface. The
ancient Greeks and Romans were among the first
people to use these minerals for decoration.
Peridot is the gem-quality variety of olivine.

**HARDNESS**  6.5–7    **SG**  3.3–4.3

**COLOUR**  Green, yellow, brown, white, or black

**TRANSPARENCY**
Transparent to translucent

**LUSTRE**  Glassy

The gold throne in Topkapi Palace, Istanbul, is decorated with 955 peridots.

## Natrolite

Natrolite takes its name from the Greek *natrium*, which means "soda" – a reference to its sodium content. It is found in cavities, volcanic ash deposits, and as veins in some rocks.

**HARDNESS** 5–5.5

**SG** 2.3

**COLOUR** Pale pink, colourless, white, grey, red, yellow, or green

**TRANSPARENCY** Transparent to translucent

**LUSTRE** Glassy to pearly

## Scapolite

Previously known as wernerite and dipyre, this silicate is known for its large crystals. The largest ones usually grow in marble.

**HARDNESS** 5–6     **SG** 2.5–2.7

**COLOUR** Colourless, white, grey, yellow, orange, or pink

**TRANSPARENCY** Transparent to opaque

**LUSTRE** Glassy

## Diopside

Diopside is found in metamorphic rocks that were once limestones or dolomites, and in some igneous rocks such as kimberlite. The mineral occurs in the rocks of the Tyrol mountains in Austria and Italy, and in the USA.

| | |
|---|---|
| **HARDNESS** 6 | |
| **SG** 3.3 | |
| **COLOUR** White, pale to dark green, violet-blue | |
| **TRANSPARENCY** Transparent to translucent | |
| **LUSTRE** Glassy | |

## Rhodonite

This silicate was named for its colour from the Greek word *rhodon*, meaning "rose". Rhodonite is widely used in making beads and jewellery, even though it is fragile and has to be carefully polished.

| | |
|---|---|
| **HARDNESS** 6 | **SG** 3.5–3.7 |
| **COLOUR** Pink to rose-red | |
| **TRANSPARENCY** Translucent | |
| **LUSTRE** Glassy | |

## Jadeite

Jadeite is one of the two minerals that are commonly called jade. The other variety is nephrite. For the ancient Indians, jadeite was a symbol of life, and regarded as precious as gold. Burma (Myanmar) is a major source of the mineral and ancient jadeite tools have been found there.

| | |
|---|---|
| **HARDNESS** 6–7 | **SG** 3.2–3.4 |
| **COLOUR** White, green, lilac, pink, brown, orange, yellow, red, blue, or black | |
| **TRANSPARENCY** Transparent to translucent | |
| **LUSTRE** Glassy to greasy | |

## Augite

This mineral is commonly found in dark-coloured igneous rocks. It also occurs in some metamorphic rocks and meteorites, and can even be found on the Moon.

| | |
|---|---|
| **HARDNESS** 5.5–6 | **SG** 3.3 |
| **COLOUR** Greenish-black to black, dark green, brown | |
| **TRANSPARENCY** Translucent to nearly opaque | |
| **LUSTRE** Glassy to dull | |

## Richterite

Richterite is a rare manganese stone usually found in igneous rocks and limestones. It was named after the German mineralogist Theodore Richter in 1865. It is mainly used for decorative purposes.

**HARDNESS** 5–6

**SG** 3–3.5

**COLOUR** Brown, yellow, red, or green

**TRANSPARENCY** Transparent to translucent

**LUSTRE** Glassy

## Hornblende

Recent studies have discovered that hornblende is a group of minerals and not a single form of a mineral. However, only detailed analysis can tell them all apart. Hornblende may occur with ruby in the Harts Range mountains in Australia.

**HARDNESS** 5–6

**SG** 3.1–3.3

**COLOUR** Green, black

**TRANSPARENCY** Translucent to opaque

**LUSTRE** Glassy

## Nephrite

Nephrite's tight interlocking fibres make it a hard rock, suitable for carving. It is named after the Latin word *nephrus*, meaning "kidney", as it was used to treat kidney diseases.

**HARDNESS** 6.5

**SG** 2.9–3.4

**COLOUR** Cream, light to dark green

**TRANSPARENCY** Translucent to nearly opaque

**LUSTRE** Dull to waxy

## Riebeckite

This mineral was once valued for its fireproofing qualities and its ability to withstand electricity and acid, but scientists later discovered that the fibres are harmful to people and caused diseases.

**HARDNESS** 6

**SG** 3.3–3.4

**COLOUR** Dark blue, black

**TRANSPARENCY** Transparent to translucent

**LUSTRE** Glassy, silky

## Emerald

The green variety of the mineral beryl is known as emerald. To the Egyptians, it was a symbol of fertility and life. The finest emeralds, such as those in the British Crown Jewels, come from Colombia, where they have been mined for centuries.

| HARDNESS | 7.5–8 |
|---|---|
| **SG** | 2.6–3 |
| **COLOUR** | Green |
| **TRANSPARENCY** | Transparent to translucent |
| **LUSTRE** | Glassy |

## Cordierite

This mineral was named after French geologist Pierre L A Cordier. Gem-quality cordierite is also called "water sapphire" after its blue colour.

| HARDNESS | 7–7.5 | **SG** | 2.6 |
|---|---|---|---|
| **COLOUR** | Blue, blue-green, grey-violet | | |
| **TRANSPARENCY** | Transparent to translucent | | |
| **LUSTRE** | Glassy to greasy | | |

## Vesuvianite

The crystals of vesuvianite are cut and polished for collectors but the transparent variety is too soft to wear. It forms when limestone undergoes changes due to heat and pressure.

| HARDNESS | 6.5 |
|---|---|
| **SG** | 3.4 |
| **COLOUR** | Green, yellow |
| **TRANSPARENCY** | Transparent to translucent |
| **LUSTRE** | Glassy to resinous |

# emimorphite

*Rounded
masses, usually
colourless*

emimorphite gets its name from the Greek
*mi*, meaning "half", and *morphe,* meaning
rm", which is a reference to its unique crystal
rm. The two ends of each crystal are of different
apes, which is quite rare in minerals.

| HARDNESS 4.5–5 | SG 3.4–3.5 |
|---|---|
| **COLOUR** Colourless, white, yellow, blue, or green | |
| **TRANSPARENCY** Transparent to translucent | |
| **LUSTRE** Glassy | |

## Talc

One of Earth's softest minerals, talc is ground finely to make talcum powder. It is the main ingredient of soapstone and has been traditionally carved to make ornaments. Talc is also used in paints and for making paper.

| HARDNESS 1 | SG 2.8 |
| --- | --- |

**COLOUR** White, colourless, green, yellow to brown

**TRANSPARENCY** Translucent

**LUSTRE** Pearly to greasy

## Muscovite

## Pyrophyllite

The name of this mineral is based on the Greek words for "fire" and "leaf" because it sheds thin, leaflike layers when heated. It provides a sheen to lipsticks and is also used as a filler in paints and rubber and in dusting powders. The ancient Chinese carved it into small images and ornaments.

| HARDNESS 1–2 | SG 2.7–2.9 |
| --- | --- |

**COLOUR** White, colourless, brown-green, pale blue, grey

**TRANSPARENCY** Transparent to translucent

**LUSTRE** Pearly to dull

Muscovite forms flat sheets and, though it looks brittle, is a tough mineral. It is also called isinglass – a reference to its use in window panes in Russia. It is a member of the mica group of minerals.

| | |
|---|---|
| **HARDNESS** 2.5 | |
| **SG** 2.8 | |

**COLOUR** Colourless, silver-white, pale green, rose, brown

**TRANSPARENCY** Transparent to translucent

**LUSTRE** Glassy

## Biotite

Biotite is also called black mica because of its iron content and dark colour. It is abundant in igneous and metamorphic rocks. Like muscovite, it splits into thin sheets.

| | |
|---|---|
| **HARDNESS** 2.5–3 | **SG** 2.7–3.4 |

**COLOUR** Black, brown, pale yellow, tan, or bronze

**TRANSPARENCY** Transparent to translucent

**LUSTRE** Glassy to submetallic

## Serpentine

There are 16 varieties of serpentine, which is named for its snakeskin-like texture. Serpentine was carved into vases and bowls on the island of Crete by the Minoans around 3,000–1,100 BCE.

**HARDNESS** 3.5–5.5

**SG** 2.5–2.6

**COLOUR** White, grey, yellow, green, or greenish-blue

**TRANSPARENCY** Translucent to opaque

**LUSTRE** Glassy to greasy, resinous, earthy, dull

## Chrysocolla

*Fine texture*

The Greek philosopher Theophrastus used the term "chrysocolla" to refer to various materials used to bind together pieces of gold. *Chrysos* is "gold" and *kola* is "glue" in Greek. The mineral is found worldwide.

| HARDNESS 2–4 | SG 2–2.4 |
|---|---|
| COLOUR Blue, blue-green | |
| TRANSPARENCY Translucent to nearly opaque | |
| LUSTRE Glassy to earthy | |

## Apophyllite

Once thought to be a single mineral, apophyllite is now known to have two varieties. Both separate into layers when heated. Colourless and green specimens from India are sometimes cut and polished as collector's gems. Crystals up to 20 cm (8 in) long are found in Bento Gonsalves, Brazil.

*Blocklike crystals*

**RDNESS** 4.5–5

2.3–2.4

**LOUR** Colourless pink, green, or yellow

**ANSPARENCY** Transparent to translucent

**STRE** Glassy

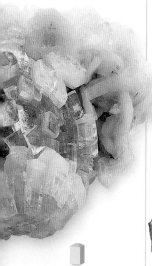

## Prehnite

Named after its discoverer Hendrik von Prehn, a Dutch military officer, prehnite is often found lining cavities in volcanic rocks. It is commonly found with the mineral zeolite and the two may be confused with one another. Transparent prehnite from Australia and Scotland is a collector's item. It is also sold under the name Cape emerald.

**HARDNESS** 6–6.5    **SG** 2.9

**COLOUR** Green, yellow, tan, or white

**TRANSPARENCY** Transparent to translucent

**LUSTRE** Glassy

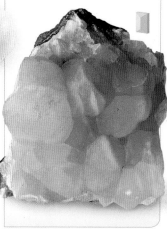

# Organic gems

Organic gems form when living things
or the substances they give off fossilize
over a long period of time. They are softer
than rock gems and so have been used
as decorative items since ancient times.

FOCUS ON...
**PEARLS**
Different types of pea[r]
form depending on
the shellfish and
its environment.

## Amber

Amber is the fossilized resin or sap of
conifer trees. Sometimes it contains trapped
insects. Mostly transparent, some pieces of
amber are cloudy due to the air trapped inside.
Its softness allows it to be carved into jewellery.

| | |
|---|---|
| **HARDNESS** | 2–2.5 |
| **SG** | 1.1 |
| **COLOUR** | Yellow, sometimes brownish or reddish |
| **TRANSPARENCY** | Transparent to translucent |
| **LUSTRE** | Resinous |

## Coral

Coral comes from the skeletons
of tiny sea animals. It can be polished to
bring out its beautiful colours, and is easily
carved into figures or beads. The most
valuable coral is red.

| | | | |
|---|---|---|---|
| **HARDNESS** | 3.5 | **SG** | 2.6-2.7 |
| **COLOUR** | Red, pink, black, blue, golden | | |
| **TRANSPARENCY** | Opaque | | |
| **LUSTRE** | Dull to glassy | | |

reshwater pearls come from
sels. They are attached to
shell and so are flat on one
 when removed.

▲ Marine-cultured pearls
are grown in the sea using
oyster shells and often have
uniform shapes and sizes.

▲ Mother of pearl is a hard layer
that lines the insides of some
shellfish. It has been used for
making utensils for a long time.

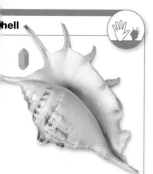

## hell

s is a hard covering found on many molluscs.
ells are made of calcite, which shellfish take
rom sea water. They are used in inlays,
ads, and in other decorative items.

| RDNESS | 2.5 | SG | About 1.3 |
|---|---|---|---|
| LOUR | Red, pink, brown, blue, golden | | |
| ANSPARENCY | Translucent to opaque | | |
| STRE | Dull to glassy | | |

## Pearl

Pearl forms in certain shellfish,
especially oysters. Gem-quality pearls come
from oysters of tropical seas. The best and the
most valuable pearls are perfectly round, but
many are egg- or pear-shaped.

| HARDNESS | 3 | SG | 2.7 |
|---|---|---|---|
| COLOUR | White, cream, black, blue, yellow, green, or pink | | |
| TRANSPARENCY | Opaque | | |
| LUSTRE | Pearly | | |

Blister pearls

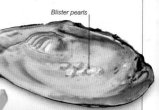

Dominican amber is around
**25 million** years old

**AMBER**
Resin from trees often traps insects and plant remains, which may become fossilized over time as the resin hardens into amber. Fossil remains found in Dominican amber can help us to understand the ecosystem of the tropical forests that existed long ago.

# The periodic table

Minerals and rocks are made up of elements – pure, naturally occurring substances that cannot be broken down further. Each element is made up of atoms. The atoms in different elements contain different amounts of particles called protons, neutrons, and electrons, which affects their chemistry. Elements are arranged in a system called the periodic table according to their chemical and physical properties.

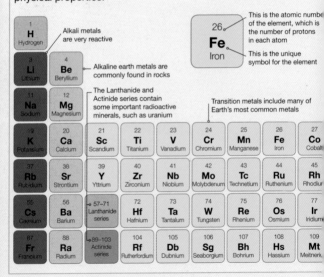

26

**Fe**
Iron

This is the atomic number of the element, which is the number of protons in each atom

This is the unique symbol for the element

1
**H**
Hydrogen

Alkali metals are very reactive

3
**Li**
Lithium

4
**Be**
Beryllium

Alkaline earth metals are commonly found in rocks

11
**Na**
Sodium

12
**Mg**
Magnesium

The Lanthanide and Actinide series contain some important radioactive minerals, such as uranium

Transition metals include many of Earth's most common metals

| 19 **K** Potassium | 20 **Ca** Calcium | 21 **Sc** Scandium | 22 **Ti** Titanium | 23 **V** Vanadium | 24 **Cr** Chromium | 25 **Mn** Manganese | 26 **Fe** Iron | 27 **Co** Cobalt |
| 37 **Rb** Rubidium | 38 **Sr** Strontium | 39 **Y** Yttrium | 40 **Zr** Zirconium | 41 **Nb** Niobium | 42 **Mo** Molybdenum | 43 **Tc** Technetium | 44 **Ru** Ruthenium | 45 **Rh** Rhodium |
| 55 **Cs** Caesium | 56 **Ba** Barium | 57–71 Lanthanide series | 72 **Hf** Hafnium | 73 **Ta** Tantalum | 74 **W** Tungsten | 75 **Re** Rhenium | 76 **Os** Osmium | 77 **Ir** Iridium |
| 87 **Fr** Francium | 88 **Ra** Radium | 89–103 Actinide series | 104 **Rf** Rutherfordium | 105 **Db** Dubnium | 106 **Sg** Seaborgium | 107 **Bh** Bohrium | 108 **Hs** Hassium | 109 **Mt** Meitnerium |

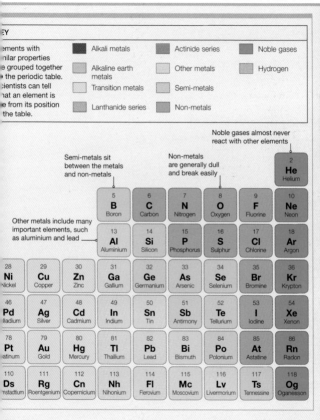

**KEY**

elements with
similar properties
re grouped together
in the periodic table.
Scientists can tell
that an element is
like from its position
in the table.

- Alkali metals
- Alkaline earth metals
- Transition metals
- Lanthanide series
- Actinide series
- Other metals
- Semi-metals
- Non-metals
- Noble gases
- Hydrogen

Noble gases almost never react with other elements

Semi-metals sit between the metals and non-metals

Non-metals are generally dull and break easily

| | | | | | | | | 2<br>**He**<br>Helium |
|---|---|---|---|---|---|---|---|---|

| 5<br>**B**<br>Boron | 6<br>**C**<br>Carbon | 7<br>**N**<br>Nitrogen | 8<br>**O**<br>Oxygen | 9<br>**F**<br>Fluorine | 10<br>**Ne**<br>Neon |
|---|---|---|---|---|---|

Other metals include many important elements, such as aluminium and lead

| 13<br>**Al**<br>Aluminium | 14<br>**Si**<br>Silicon | 15<br>**P**<br>Phosphorus | 16<br>**S**<br>Sulphur | 17<br>**Cl**<br>Chlorine | 18<br>**Ar**<br>Argon |
|---|---|---|---|---|---|

| 28<br>**Ni**<br>Nickel | 29<br>**Cu**<br>Copper | 30<br>**Zn**<br>Zinc | 31<br>**Ga**<br>Gallium | 32<br>**Ge**<br>Germanium | 33<br>**As**<br>Arsenic | 34<br>**Se**<br>Selenium | 35<br>**Br**<br>Bromine | 36<br>**Kr**<br>Krypton |
|---|---|---|---|---|---|---|---|---|
| 46<br>**Pd**<br>Palladium | 47<br>**Ag**<br>Silver | 48<br>**Cd**<br>Cadmium | 49<br>**In**<br>Indium | 50<br>**Sn**<br>Tin | 51<br>**Sb**<br>Antimony | 52<br>**Te**<br>Tellurium | 53<br>**I**<br>Iodine | 54<br>**Xe**<br>Xenon |
| 78<br>**Pt**<br>Platinum | 79<br>**Au**<br>Gold | 80<br>**Hg**<br>Mercury | 81<br>**Tl**<br>Thallium | 82<br>**Pb**<br>Lead | 83<br>**Bi**<br>Bismuth | 84<br>**Po**<br>Polonium | 85<br>**At**<br>Astatine | 86<br>**Rn**<br>Radon |
| 110<br>**Ds**<br>Darmstadtium | 111<br>**Rg**<br>Roentgenium | 112<br>**Cn**<br>Copernicium | 113<br>**Nh**<br>Nihonium | 114<br>**Fl**<br>Flerovium | 115<br>**Mc**<br>Moscovium | 116<br>**Lv**<br>Livermorium | 117<br>**Ts**<br>Tennessine | 118<br>**Og**<br>Oganesson |

# Rock facts

## LANDMARK ROCK FORMATIONS

▶ The **Rock of Gibraltar** is a huge mass of limestone at the southern tip of Spain. It rises 426 m (1,400 ft) above the sea.

▶ **Shiprock Pinnacle** in New Mexico is the remains of a 27-million-year-old volcanic vent that stands 500 m (1,640 ft) above the surrounding plain. It is considered sacred by the Navajo people.

▶ **Giant's Causeway** in Northern Ireland is a collection of 40,000 basalt pillars formed 50–60 million years ago. The tallest pillars can measure up to 25 m (82 ft) high.

▶ **Ayer's Rock**, or **Uluru**, in Australia is a giant outcrop of ancient sandstone that stands 348 m (1,142 ft) high and measures 9.4 km (5.8 miles) around its base.

▶ **Delicate Arch**, in Utah, USA, formed from weathered sandstone that has naturally eroded into a graceful arch that is 13.5 m (45 ft) high and wide enough to drive trucks through.

## METEORITES

Around 20,000 meteorites fall from space to Earth every year. Most are small, but some larger ones weigh many tonnes.

● **Willamette meteorite** was discovered in Oregon, USA, in 1902. It weighed more than 14.2 tonnes – more than the weight of three elephants.

● **Zagami meteorite** landed in Nigeria in 1962. It weighed 18 kg (40 lb) and is the largest meteorite from Mars ever found on Earth. It started as a chunk of volcanic rock on Mars that was flung into space about 2.5 million years ago when an asteroid or comet hit Mars.

A typical meteorite enters Earth's atmosphere at 10–70 km (6.2–43.5 miles) per second.

● **Y000593 meteorite** landed in Antarctica in 2000. It weighed 13.7 kg (30.2 lb), about the same as 240 eggs.

● **Sayh al Uhaymir 008** landed in Oman in 1999. It weighed 8.5 kg (18.7 lb) – as much as a small dog.

● **Nakhla meteorite** landed in El-Nakhla village, Egypt, in 1911. It weighed 5 kg (11 lb) – as much as five bags of sugar.

## OCK ELEMENTS

re than 98 per cent of all rocks in the
rld are formed from a combination of
t eight elements.

| ement | % of all rocks |
|---|---|
| ygen | 46.5 |
| con | 27.6 |
| minium | 8 |
| n | 5 |
| cium | 3.6 |
| dium | 2.8 |
| tassium | 2.6 |
| gnesium | 2 |
| tal | 98.1% |

## UILDING WITH ROCK

arge building, such as a bank or town
l, can be like a rock museum – it's a
ance to see how useful rocks are in
eryday life.

 **Granite** can be used for the base
 walls because it is very tough.

 The columns and steps of
 trances are often made with
 ite **limestone**.

 Important buildings often
 ve floors of **marble**
 cause it looks beautiful
 en polished.

## CLAY

Clay is a versatile sedimentary rock that
is used for much more than just pots.

♦ Clay is used to make ceramic tiles,
pottery, porcelain, baths, sinks, drainpipes,
bricks, and also firebricks for chimneys
and furnaces.

♦ It is used in textiles to give weight
to the fabric, and in paper-making to
give paper a gloss.

♦ Wild macaws often peck on clay at
riverbanks. It helps them to digest the
poisons in some of the seeds they eat.

♦ Elephants lick clay from mud holes.
This helps them to digest leaves they
have eaten during the day.

♦ Kaolinite is a type of clay used in many
indigestion remedies for people.

♦ Clay helps soil to retain the fertilizer
chemicals it obtains from manure,
and also helps plants to grow by
absorbing ammonia and other
gases. However, too much
clay will make the soil
heavy, preventing water
and air from seeping in.

♦ Fuller's earth is a clay
material used to purify fats.

Most rocks are hard
and stiff, but a few are
flexible. A rare type
of sandstone found in
India can be bent
in your hands.

# Mineral facts

## MOST VALUABLE DIAMONDS

**Koh-i-Noor** is the largest and purest diamond in the world. It weighs 109 carats (21.8 g/0.77 oz) and is considered priceless.

The **Sancy diamond** was once owned by the Great Mughals of India. This priceless diamond weighs 55.23 carats (11.05 g/0.39 oz).

The **Cullinan** diamond is valued at $400 million. It was found in 1905 and weighed 3,106.75 carats (621.35 g/ 21.9 oz) before being cut into 9 large and 96 smaller stones.

The **Hope diamond** weighs 45.52 carats (9.1 g/0.32 oz) and is worth $350 million – but is said to bring bad luck.

## MINING FOR MINERALS

• The earliest mines were small pits and tunnels that were dug about 8,000 years ago. They were mines for flint, a rock used to make tools, spears, and arrowheads.

• The first mines for metal were dug about 5,500 years ago. Tin and copper ores were crushed and heated together to make bronze.

• The deepest mines are the gold mines of South Africa. The record holder is Western Deep Levels Mine. Some of its tunnels are 3.5 km (2.2 miles) below the surface.

• Not all mines are holes in the ground. Along the coast of Namibia, Africa, large ships vacuum up sand from the ocean floor and sift it for diamonds.

## HEALING MINERALS

People have believed for thousands of years that the crystals of certain minerals can help heal the body and calm the mind, and bring good luck.

**Rose quartz** brings unconditional love.

**Lapis lazuli** promotes friendship.

**Jade** brings relaxation.

**Bloodstone** increases creativity and intuition.

**Onyx** changes bad habits.

**Hematite** relieves the stress of air travel.

**Amethyst** cures acne.

# USEFUL MINERALS

Minerals make up 99 per cent of Earth's crust. Many are valuable and are used to make items that we need every day.

★ Aluminium is the most abundant metal found in minerals, including **bauxite** and **gibbite**. It is used to make cans and in the construction of buildings.

★ Antimony comes from the mineral **stibnite**. It is used to harden lead in batteries and cables, and to make fireworks and glass.

★ **Chromite** is a source of the metal chromium, which is used to harden steel and make machine tools, ball bearings, and kitchen utensils.

★ Copper is used in electric wires and cables, in plumbing and in kitchen utensils. It is also used to make alloys such as brass (a mixture of copper and zinc) and bronze (copper and tin). **Chalcopyrite** is the main source of copper.

★ **Feldspar** is the one of Earth's most common minerals. It is used in making glass and ceramics, and in soaps, abrasives, cement, and concrete.

★ **Fluorspar** is used to make acid for the production of non-stick coatings on pans. It is also used in toothpaste.

★ Iron is a metal found in minerals such as **hematite**. It is used to make steel, magnets, and car parts.

★ Lead is a metal found in the mineral **galena** and is used to make batteries and television tubes.

★ Limestone is a rock made mostly of the mineral **calcite**. It is used in the construction of buildings and in making cement, paper, plastic, and glass.

★ Manganese is used in making steel, and in dyes, alloys, and batteries. It is obtained from ore minerals including **pyrolusite**.

★ **Mica** is a group of important minerals that are used in paints, plastics, and rubber.

★ **Nickel** is a native element that is used to make stainless steel.

★ The native element **silver** is used to make jewellery, cutlery, and coins.

There are more than 4,500 known minerals in the world. Only 100 are common – the rest are rarer than gold.

# GLOSSARY

**Acid** A chemical that contains a reactive form of the hydrogen atom. This readily attacks other chemicals.

**Atom** The basic unit of an element.

**Adamantine lustre** A particularly brilliant shine as shown by diamond.

**Asteroid** A chunk of rock smaller than a planet that orbits the Sun.

**Atmosphere** The blanket of gases surrounding Earth or another planet.

**Bed** A thin layer of sedimentary rock.

**Breccia** A sedimentary rock made up of angular fragments.

**Canyon** A deep, steep-sided valley, typically cut by a river.

**Carat** The standard measure of weight for precious stones and metals. A carat is equal to 0.2 g (0.007 oz).

**Chondrite** A stony meteorite containing tiny granules of pyroxene and olivine.

**Cleavage** The way a mineral or rock breaks along a certain plane, or in a certain direction.

**Concretions** Usually rounded, rock masses formed and found in beds of shale or clay.

**Core** Earth's hot, dense iron-rich centre – liquid on the outside and solid on the inside.

**Crystal** A naturally occurring substance whose atoms are arranged in a regular manner.

**Crystal system** The systems into which crystals are grouped based on their symmetry. There are six crystal systems: cubic, monoclinic, triclinic, trigonal/hexagonal, orthorhombic, and tetragonal.

**Crust** Earth's rigid, outermost layer. It is divided into thicker, older continental crust (mainly granite) and thinner, more recent oceanic crust (mainly basalt).

**Detrital** A type of sediment that has settled in water or has been deposited by water.

**Dull lustre** A shine that reflects very little.

**Dyke** A thin, sheetlike igneous intrusion that cuts across older rock structures.

**Dynamic pressure** The process by which an existing rock changes due to pressure alone to form metamorphic rocks.

**Earthy lustre** A non-reflective mineral lustre.

**Element** A substance that cannot be broken down further.

**Erosion** A slow process in which rocks are worn away by moving water, ice, and wind.

**Eruption** A discharge of lava, ash, or gas from a volcanic cone or vent.

**Evaporite** A natural salt or mineral left behind after the water it was dissolved in has dried up.

**Extrusive rock** A rock that forms when lava flows onto Earth's surface, cools, and solidifies.

**Faces** The external flat surfaces that make up a crystal's shape.

**Fault** An extended fracture in rock along which rock masses move.

**Fluorescence** The optical effect whereby a mineral appears a different colour in ultraviolet light than in ordinary daylight.

**Foliation** A pattern formed when different minerals separate within a metamorphic rock.

**Fold** Bends in rock strata (layers) caused by the movement of tectonic plates.

**Fossil** Any record of past life preserved in rocks, including bones, shells, footprints, and dung.

**Fracture** The distinctive way in which a mineral breaks.

**Gemstone** A mineral, usually crystal-like, which is valued for its colour, rarity, and hardness.

**Geologist** A scientist who studies Earth and its structure and composition.

**Groundmass** Compact fine-grained mineral material in which larger crystals are embedded.

**Habit** The general shape of a mineral.

**Hydrothermal vein** A crack in rock through which hot mineral waters circulate due to volcanic activity. As the waters cool, minerals start to crystallize, forming gemstones and ores.

**usive rock** A
k that forms when
gma solidifies below
h's crust.

**eous rock** A
k formed from
dification of
a or magma
or below
th's surface.

**escence** A play
colours that looks
oil on water that
urs when light
ects off internal
ments of a rock
mineral.

**a** Magma that
flowed onto
h's surface
ough a volcanic
ning.

**stre** The way in
ch light reflects off
surface of a mineral.

**gma** Molten rock
d deep inside Earth.

**ntle** The middle
er of Earth,
ween the core
I the crust.
onsists of hot,
se rocks, such
peridotite.

**tallic lustre** A
ne like that of
ished metal.

**tamorphic rock**
ck formed when
er rocks are
nsformed by heat,
pressure, or both.

**Meteor** A meteoroid
(rock and dust debris in
space) that enters Earth's
atmosphere and appears
as a shooting star.

**Meteorite** A meteoroid
that reaches the surface
of Earth.

**Mineral** A naturally
occurring solid with
specific characteristics,
such as a particular
chemical composition
and crystal shape.

**Mineralogist** A scientist
who studies minerals.

**Native element** A
chemical element found
in nature in its pure form.

**Nodule** A hard, rounded,
stony lump found in
sedimentary rock, typically
made from calcite, silica,
pyrite, or gypsum.

**Oolitic** A rock that forms
from ooliths, which are
individual round grains of
sediment. Most ooliths
are made of calcite.

**Opaque** A substance
or material that does not
let light pass through it.

**Ore** A rock or mineral
from which a metal
can be extracted.

**Organic** Relating to
living things.

**Prism** A solid geometric
figure with a set of faces
parallel to one another.

**Pluton** Any body of
intrusive igneous rock.

**Quarry** A place where
stone is dug up.

**Regional change** The
process by which an
existing rock changes
due to heat and
pressure to form
metamorphic rocks.

**Resinous lustre** A
shine like that of resin.

**Rock** A solid mixture
of minerals. There are
three types: igneous,
metamorphic, and
sedimentary.

**Secondary mineral**
A mineral that replaces
another as a result of
weathering or other
alteration process.

**Sediments** Particles
of rock, mineral, or
organic matter that
are deposited by wind,
water, and ice.

**Sedimentary rock**
A rock formed from
sediments that have
been cemented
together by weathering
or burial.

**Semi-metal** A chemical
element that shares some
properties with metals and
some with non-metals.

**Sill** A thin, sheetlike,
igneous intrusion that
forms between layers
of existing rocks.

**Specific gravity** The
ratio of a mineral's
weight compared to
the weight of an equal
volume of water.

**Streak** The colour of
a mineral's powder.
It is less variable than
the colour of mineral,
so is a more reliable
identification tool.

**Tectonic plate** One of
about 12 huge, floating
rock slabs that make up
the rigid outer layer of
Earth's crust.

**Thermal contact** The
process by which an
existing rock changes
due to heat alone to
form metamorphic rock.

**Uplift** The result of
rock structures being
raised upwards by the
movement of tectonic
plates. Sediments
formed on the sea
bed may be uplifted
to become mountains.

**Vitreous lustre** A shine
like that of glass.

**Volcano** The site of an
eruption of lava and hot
gases from within Earth.
Magma flows up a
central passage and
erupts as lava.

**Weathering** The slow
breakdown of rock by
long exposure to the
weather, including
moisture, frost,
and rainwater.

# Index

# Acknowledgments

Dorling Kindersley would like to thank: Monica Byles for proofreading; Helen Peters for indexing; David Roberts and Rob Campbell for database creation; Claire Bowers, Fabian Harry, Romaine Werblow, and Rose Horridge for DK Picture Library assistance; Ritu Mishra, Nasreen Habib, Neha Chaudhary, Deeksha Saikia, Jessica Cawthra, Kingshuk Ghoshal, and Francesca Baines for editorial assistance; Isha Nagar, Revati Anand, Chrissy Barnard, Govind Mittal, and Philip Letsu for design assistance; Saloni Singh for the jacket; Bimlesh Tiwary, Dheeraj Singh, Jaypal Singh, Pawan Kumar, Balwant Singh, and Rakesh Kumar for DTP assistance; Deepak Negi for picture research assistance; and David Almond for pre-production.

The publishers would also like to thank the following for their kind permission to reproduce their photographs:

(Key: a-above; b-below/bottom; c-centre; f-far; l-left; r-right; t-top)

2–3 Corbis: Walter Geiersperger (c). 5 Getty Images: Toshi Sasaki / Stone+ (tr); Science & Society Picture Library (tc). 6 Dorling Kindersley: Natural History Museum, London (ca). Getty Images: Siede Preis / Photodisc (bl). 7 Alamy Images: E D Torial (b). Dorling Kindersley: Natural History Museum, London (tl, cr). Getty Images: f8 Imaging / Hulton Archive (tr). 8–9 Science Photo Library: Dirk Wiersma (c). 10 Alamy Images: Tom Grundy (cl). Dorling Kindersley: Natural History Museum, London (br). 11 Dorling Kindersley: Natural History Museum, London (tl, br). 12 Dorling Kindersley: Natural History Museum,
London (tc). 12–13 Dorling Kindersley: Natural History Museum, London (c). 14 Corbis: Frans Lanting. 15 Corbis: Atlantide Phototravel. 18 Dorling Kindersley: Oxford University Museum of Natural History (cl). 19 Dorling Kindersley: Natural History Museum, London (bl). 20 Dorling Kindersley: Natural History Museum, London (cl). 21 Corbis: Granville Harris / Eye Ubiquitous (tl). Getty Images: Jeff Foott / Discovery Channel Images (tc). 24–25 Dorling Kindersley: Natural History Museum, London (b). 28–29 Dreamstime.com: Natalia Bratslavsky. 30 Dorling Kindersley: Judith Miller / Freeman's (tl); Natural History Museum, London (bl, bl/Powdered Clay). 32 Dorling Kindersley: Natural History Museum, London (tl). 40–41 Alamy Images: Pritz / F1online digitale Bildagentur GmbH. 42 Dorling Kindersley: Rough Guides (tl). 50–51 Getty Images: Andreas Strauss / LOOK. 54 Dorling Kindersley: The Smithsonian Institution, Washington DC. 55 Dorling Kindersley: Judith Miller / 333 Auctions LLC. 56 Dorling Kindersley: Natural History Museum, London (c). 56–57 Alamy Images: Photoshot Holdings Ltd (b). 57 Dorling Kindersley: Natural History Museum, London (b). 58 Dorling Kindersley: Natural History Museum, London (tl, br). 62 Dorling Kindersley: Oxford University Museum of Natural History (br). 63 Dorling Kindersley: Natural History Museum, London (tl). 65 Dorling Kindersley: Natural History Museum, London (c, br). 66 Dorling Kindersley: Natural History Museum, London (tl). 67 Corbis: Corbis Art (t). Dorling Kindersley: Natural History Museum, London (bc). Getty Images: Tim Graham (cr). 68 Dorling Kindersley: Natural History Museum,
London (br); The Science Museum, London (cl). NASA: Human Spaceflight Collection (bl). 71 Dorling Kindersley: Oxford University Museum of Natural History (tr). 73 Dorling Kindersley: Natural History Museum, London. 74–75 Getty Images: Radius Images. 76 Getty Images: Dea / A Dagli Orti (cl); Steve Eason / Hulton Archive (tl). 77 Dorling Kindersley: Natural History Museum, London (cl). 88–89 Getty Images: Peter Ginter / Science Faction. 90 Alamy Images: De Schuyter Marc / Arterra Picture Library (tl). Corbis: Macduff Everton (cl). SuperStock: imagebroker.net (bl). 92 Dorling Kindersley: Natural History Museum, London (br). 102–103 Corbis: Bertrand Gardel / Hemis. 114–115 Corbis: Randy Faris. 119 Dorling Kindersley: Dan Bannister (tl). 122 Dorling Kindersley: Judith Miller / Blanchet et Associes (tl); Judith Miller / Sylvie Spectrum (cl); Judith Miller / Lynn & Brian Holmes (tr). 124 Dorling Kindersley: The Smithsonian Institution, Washington DC (tl). 127 Dorling Kindersley: Natural History Museum, London (tr). 132 Dorling Kindersley: Natural History Museum, London (tr). 141 Dorling Kindersley: Natural History Museum, London (tr). 142–143 Corbis: Jeff Daly / Visuals Unlimited.

Cover images: Front: Dorling Kindersley: Natural History Museum, London c; Spine: Dorling Kindersley: Natural History Museum, London

All other images © Dorling Kindersley

For further information see:
www.dkimages.com